Psychology: A Very Short Introduction

VERY SHORT INTRODUCTIONS are for anyone wanting a stimulating and accessible way in to a new subject. They are written by experts, and have been translated into more than 40 different languages.

The Series began in 1995, and now covers a wide variety of topics in every discipline. The VSI library now contains over 350 volumes—a Very Short Introduction to everything from Psychology and Philosophy of Science to American History and Relativity—and continues to grow in every subject area.

## Very Short Introductions available now:

Available soon:

For more information visit our website
www.oup.com/vsi/

Gillian Butler and Freda McManus

# PSYCHOLOGY

A Very Short Introduction

OXFORD
UNIVERSITY PRESS

# OXFORD
UNIVERSITY PRESS

Great Clarendon Street, Oxford, OX2 6DP,
United Kingdom

Oxford University Press is a department of the University of Oxford.
It furthers the University's objective of excellence in research, scholarship,
and education by publishing worldwide. Oxford is a registered trade mark of
Oxford University Press in the UK and in certain other countries

© Gillian Butler and Freda McManus 2014

The moral rights of the authors have been asserted

First published 1998
Reissued 2000
Second Edition published 2014

Published in the United States of America by Oxford University Press
198 Madison Avenue, New York, NY 10016, United States of America

British Library Cataloguing in Publication Data
Data available

Library of Congress Control Number: 2013947883

ISBN 978-0-19-967042-0

Printed and bound by
CPI Group (UK) Ltd, Croydon, CR0 4YY

# Contents

# Acknowledgements

It has been a pleasure to immerse ourselves again in the fascinating and fast-developing world of psychology while writing a new edition of this *Very Short Introduction*, and we are immensely grateful to Stephanie Burnett Heyes for helping with this process. She pointed us in the direction of new findings that we might otherwise have missed, and helped us to keep current approaches to the subject in mind while we focused on providing a snapshot of the subject that accurately reflects its history, its enduring concerns, and developments in new fields such as those of cognitive neuropsychology, Internet technology, and methods of qualitative as well as quantitative data collection and analysis.

Patients, students, colleagues, friends, and family have all played their part in helping us to think clearly about psychology, and we are grateful to them all. The many questions that they have posed have helped us to focus on aspects of psychology that are of general interest. They have also challenged us to provide answers that reveal the exciting nature of psychology as a developing science, that fit with a fast expanding set of facts, and that can be relatively simply explained and illustrated. Inevitably we have had to leave unexplored, or merely hint at the existence of, large parts of the territory. We are grateful to those whose curiosity helped to point us in directions that they found interesting.

We would particularly like to thank our original teachers of psychology for imparting an enduring enthusiasm for the subject, and also those whose writings have helped us to think better about how to make the science of psychology accessible to others. The works of some of these have been included amongst the selection of further reading that we have recommended at the end of the book.

It is also a pleasure to acknowledge the high quality of the work done by the editorial team at Oxford University Press in the process of producing this new edition. Any remaining errors are ours. Our main wish is to convey an interest and enthusiasm for this subject that is not only ours but is shared by those who have helped us along the way.

# List of illustrations

Psychology

The publisher and author apologize for any errors or omissions in the above list. If contacted they will be happy to rectify these at the earliest opportunity.

# Chapter 1
# What is psychology? How do you study it?

In 1890 William James (Figure 1), the American philosopher and physician and one of the founders of modern psychology, defined psychology as 'the science of mental life' and this definition can still provide a starting point for our understanding today. We all have a mental life and therefore have some idea about what this means, even though it can be studied in rats or monkeys as well as in people. However it is only a starting point. New ways of studying the brain, and of understanding its structure and workings, provide us with fascinating information about the determinants of our mental lives. Improved technology means that activity in the brain can now be objectively observed and measured. However, there is much we do not know about the relationships between subjective experience and the brain, and psychologists are still making hypotheses, or informed guesses, about how the two kinds of knowledge—the subjective and the objective—are linked.

Like most psychologists, William James was particularly interested in human psychology, which he thought consisted of certain basic elements: thoughts and feelings, a physical world which exists in time and space, and a way of knowing about these things. For each of us, this knowledge comes from our individual interactions with the world and from the thoughts and feelings linked with these experiences. For this reason, it is easy for us to

1. William James (1842–1910)

make judgements about psychological matters using our own experience as a touchstone. We behave as amateur psychologists when we offer opinions on complex psychological phenomena, such as whether brain-washing works, or when we express opinions about why other people behave as they do—for example, thinking they are being insulted; feeling unhappy; or suddenly giving up their jobs. However, problems arise when two people understand these things differently. Formal psychology attempts to provide methods for deciding which explanations are most likely to be correct, or for determining the circumstances under which each applies. The work of psychologists helps us to distinguish between inside information which is subjective, and objective facts: between our preconceptions and what is true in scientific terms.

Psychology, as defined by William James, is about the mind. Until recently it was not possible to study the living human brain directly, so psychologists studied our behaviour, and used their observations to derive hypotheses about what is going on inside. Now our knowledge of the workings of the brain has increased, and provides a scientific basis for understanding some aspects of our mental life. This is exciting, but there is still more to be discovered before we can claim to be able to explain variations in the experience and expression of our hopes, fears, and wishes, or in our behaviour during experiences as varied as giving birth and watching a football match. Psychology is also about the ways in which organisms, usually people, use their mental abilities, or minds, to operate in the world around them. The ways in which they do this have changed over time as their social and physical environment has changed. Evolutionary theory suggests that if organisms do not adapt to a changing environment they will become extinct (hence the sayings 'adapt or die' and 'survival of the fittest'). We have been, and still are being, shaped by adaptive processes. This means that there are evolutionary explanations for the ways in which our brains, and our minds, work. For instance, the reason we are better at detecting moving objects

3

than those that are stationary may be because this ability was useful in helping our ancestors to avoid predators. It is important for psychologists, as it is for other scientists, to be aware of those reasons.

A difficulty inherent in the study of psychology is that scientific facts should be objective and verifiable, but the workings of the mind are not observable in the way that those of an engine are. Scientists have only been able to study them in detail since they have developed numerous specialized and clever techniques, a few of which are described in this book. In everyday life they can only be perceived indirectly, and have to be inferred from what can be observed. The endeavour of psychology is much like that involved in solving a crossword puzzle. It involves evaluating and interpreting the available clues, and using what you already know to fill in the gaps. Furthermore, the clues themselves have to be derived from careful observation, based on accurate measurement, analysed with all possible scientific rigour, and interpreted using logical and reasoned arguments which can be subjected to public scrutiny. Only a part of what we want to know in psychology—how we perceive, learn, remember, think, solve problems, feel, develop, differ from each other, and interrelate—can be measured directly, and all these activities are *multiply determined*: meaning that they are influenced by several factors rather than by a single one. For example, think of all the things that may affect your response to a particular situation such as losing your way in a strange town. In order to find out which factors are important, a number of other confounding factors have somehow to be ruled out.

Complex interactions are the norm rather than the exception in psychology, and understanding them depends on the development of sophisticated techniques and theories. Psychology has the same goals as many other sciences: to describe, understand, and predict the processes that it studies. Once these goals have been achieved we can better understand the nature of our experience and make practical use of this knowledge. For instance, psychological findings have been useful in pursuits as varied as the development of more effective methods of teaching children to read, designing control panels for machines that reduce the risk of accidents, and seeking to alleviate the suffering of people who are emotionally distressed.

## Historical background

Although psychological questions have been discussed for centuries, they have only been investigated scientifically since the late 19th century. Early psychologists relied on *introspection*, that is, reflection on one's own conscious experience, to find answers to psychological questions. These early psychological investigations aimed to identify mental structures. But following the publication by Charles Darwin of *The Origin of Species* in 1859, the scope of psychology expanded to include the *functions* as well as the *structures* of consciousness. Mental structures and functions are still of central interest to psychologists today, but using introspection for studying them has obvious limitations. As Sir Francis Galton pointed out, it leaves one 'a helpless spectator of but a minute fraction of automatic brain work'. Attempting to grasp the mind through introspection, according to William James, is like 'turning up the gas quickly enough to see how the darkness looks'. Contemporary psychologists therefore base their theories on careful observations of the phenomena in which they are interested, such as the behaviour of others and the workings of their brains, rather than on reflections upon their own experience.

In 1913, John Watson published a general behaviourist manifesto for psychology which asserted that, if psychology was to be a science, the *data* on which it was based must be available for inspection. This focus on observable behaviour rather than on internal (unobservable) mental events was linked with a theory of learning and an emphasis on reliable methods of observation and experimentation which still influence psychology today.

The behaviourist approach suggests that all behaviour is the result of conditioning, which can be studied by specifying the *stimulus* and observing the *response* to it (*S–R psychology*). What happens in between these two, the *intervening variables*, was thought unimportant by the earlier behaviourists, but it has since become a prime source of experimental hypotheses. Testing these hypotheses has enabled psychologists to develop increasingly sophisticated theories about mental structures, functions, and processes.

Two other significant influences on the development of psychology early this century came from *Gestalt psychology* and from *psychoanalysis*. Gestalt psychologists working in Germany made some interesting observations about the ways in which psychological processes are organized. They showed that our experience differs from what would be expected if it were based solely on the physical properties of external stimuli, and concluded that 'the whole is greater than the sum of the parts'. For example, when two lights in close proximity flash in succession, what we see is one light that moves between the two positions (this is how films work). Recognizing that mental processes contribute in this way to the nature of experience laid the groundwork for contemporary developments in *cognitive psychology*, which is the branch of psychology that studies such internal processes.

Sigmund Freud's theories about the continuing influence of early childhood experiences, and about the theoretical psychological structures he named the *ego*, *id*, and *superego*, drew attention to *unconscious* processes. These processes, which include unconscious and unacceptable wishes and desires, are inferred, for example, from dreams, slips of the tongue, and mannerisms, and are thought to influence behaviour. In particular, unconscious conflicts are hypothesized to be a prime cause of psychological distress, which psychoanalysts try to relieve by assisting in their expression, and by offering interpretations based on their theories. These theories about unobservable mental processes, however, have not led to testable predictions, and may not be precise or specific enough to do so. Indeed, the scientific and the interpretive branches of psychology subsequently developed independently.

Contemporary psychology is at an exciting stage today partly because these divisions are, in places, breaking down. We now know much about what goes on in our minds 'out of awareness' but we use other theories to explain these findings. Psychology is not the only discipline that has had to tackle questions about how we can know about things that we cannot observe directly—think of physics and biochemistry. Technological and theoretical advances have assisted this process and such developments have changed, and are continuing to change, the nature of psychology as a science. Using sophisticated measuring instruments, electronic equipment, and improved statistical methods, psychologists can now analyse multiple variables and huge quantities of data. Observations of the brain at work, for example using fMRI scanners, and the study of the mind as an *information processing system*, have enabled them to find out about aspects of the brain and mind that could not previously be observed, and thus to specify what goes on between stimulus and response during perception, attention, thinking, and decision-making. Psychologists are now in a position to base their hypotheses about these things on data derived from *reliable* and *valid* methods of observation and accurate measurement. These developments have produced a revolution in psychology as 'the science of mental life', and have enabled psychologists to collaborate with scientists in fields as diverse as chemistry and computer science.

## Psychology as a cognitive science

Cognitive science is the interdisciplinary study of the mind and its processes, and its findings have expanded so fast that they are said to have created a 'cognitive revolution'. Figure 2 shows an adaptation of a diagram provided by George A. Miller in 2003 to illustrate the different fields—including psychology—that contributed to the birth of cognitive science. So the work of psychologists is now closely linked to that of other scientists, and contributes for instance to the scientific study of the nervous system: neuroscience. As outlined by Nobel laureate Eric Kandel, cognitive neuroscience is concerned with perception, action, memory, language, and selective attention—all of which are central subjects for psychologists. Cognitive neuro-psychology aims to understand how the structure and function of the brain relate to these psychological processes.

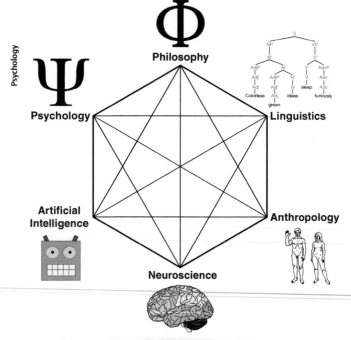

2. Fields contributing to cognitive science

However, some of the areas that interest psychologists cannot be understood by using scientific methods of investigation alone, and some would argue that they never will be. For example, the *humanistic* school of psychology places great emphasis on individuals' own accounts of their subjective experiences, and on qualitative as well as quantitative methods of analysis. Some of the main methods that are typically used by psychologists are shown in Box 1 and often these approaches can be combined to good effect. For example, quantitative methods of investigation such as the use of questionnaires can be enhanced by including a qualitative component to the research. Results from questionnaires may tell us, for example, that the patients who received treatment A improved more than those who received treatment B, but qualitative analysis through semi-structured interviews could help us to understand how treatment A helped, and how the patients were affected by each of the treatments, helping us to further refine the interventions.

Any science can only be as good as the data on which it is based. Hence psychologists must be objective in their methods of data collection, analysis, and interpretation; in their use of statistics; and in the interpretation of the results of their analyses. An example will illustrate how, even if the data collected are valid and reliable, pitfalls can easily arise in the way they are interpreted. If it is reported that 90 per cent of child abusers were abused themselves as children, it is easy to assume that most people who were abused as children will go on to become child abusers themselves—and indeed such comments often reach the media. However, the interpretation does not in fact follow logically from the information given—the majority of people who have themselves been abused do not repeat this pattern of behaviour. Psychologists, as researchers, have therefore to learn how to present their data in an objective way that is not likely to mislead, and to interpret the facts and figures reported by others. This involves a high degree of critical, scientific thinking.

## Box 1 The main methods of investigation used by psychologists

*Laboratory experiments*: a hypothesis derived from a theory is tested under controlled conditions which are intended to reduce bias in both the selection of subjects used and in the measurement of the variables being studied. Findings should be replicable but may not generalize to more real-life settings. These include observations of the brain at work.

*Field experiments*: hypotheses are tested outside laboratories, in more natural conditions, but these experiments may be less well controlled, harder to replicate, or may not generalize to other settings.

*Correlational methods*: assessing the strength of the relationship between two or more variables, such as reading level and attention span. This is a method of data analysis, rather than data collection.

*Observations of behaviour*: the behaviour in question must be clearly defined, and methods of observing it should be reliable. Observations must be truly representative of the behaviour that is of interest.

*Case studies*: particularly useful following brain damage, as a source of ideas for future research, and for measuring the same behaviour repeatedly under different conditions.

*Self-report and Questionnaire studies*: these provide subjective data, based on self-knowledge (or introspection), and their reliability can be ensured through good test design and by standardizing the tests on large representative samples.

*Surveys*: useful for collecting new ideas, and for sampling the responses of the population in which the psychologist is interested.

*Interviews*: a source of qualitative data about human behaviour which can be used to derive impressions about underlying processes.

## The main branches of psychology

It has been argued that psychology is not a science because there is no single governing paradigm or theoretical principle upon which it is based. Rather it is composed of many loosely allied schools of thought. However, this feature of psychology is perhaps inevitable because of its subject matter. Studying the physiology, biology, or chemistry of an organism provides the kind of exclusive focus that is not available to psychologists precisely *because* they are interested in mental processes, which cannot be separated from all the other aspects of the organism. So there are, as one might expect, many approaches to the study of psychology, ranging from the more artistic to the more scientific, and the different branches of the subject may seem at times like completely separate fields. The main ones are listed in Box 2. In practice there is a considerable overlap between the different branches as well as between psychology and related fields.

## Close relatives of psychology

There are some fields with which psychology is frequently confused—and for good reason.

First, psychology is not psychiatry. Psychiatry is a branch of medicine which specializes in helping people to overcome mental disorders. It therefore concentrates on what happens when things go wrong: on mental illness and mental distress. Psychologists also apply their skills in the clinic, but they are not medical doctors and they combine a wide knowledge of normal psychological processes and development with their focus on psychological problems and distress. They are not usually able to prescribe drugs; rather they specialize in helping people to understand, control, or modify their thoughts or behaviour in order to reduce their suffering and distress.

## Box 2 The main branches of psychology

*Abnormal*: the study of psychological dysfunctions and of ways of overcoming them.

*Behavioural*: emphasizes behaviour, learning, and the collection of data which can be directly observed.

*Biological (and comparative)*: the study of the psychology of different species, inheritance patterns, and determinants of behaviour.

*Cognitive*: focuses on finding out how information is collected, processed, understood, and used.

*Developmental*: how organisms change during their lifespan.

*Individual differences*: studying large groups of people so as to identify and understand typical variations, for example in intelligence or personality.

*Physiological*: focuses on the mutual influences between physiological state and psychology, and on the workings of the senses, nervous system, and brain.

*Social*: studying social behaviour, and interactions between individuals and groups.

Second, psychology is often confused with psychotherapy. Psychotherapy is a broad term referring to many different types of psychological therapy, but referring to no particular type exclusively. Although the term is often used to refer to psychodynamic and humanistic approaches to therapy, it also has a wider, more general use; for example, there has recently been a great expansion in cognitive-behavioural psychotherapy.

Third, there are many related fields, in addition to neuro-psychology, in which psychologists may work, or collaborate with others, including psychometrics, psycho-physiology, and psycho-linguistics. Psychologists also play a part in broader, developing fields to which others contribute as well, such as cognitive science and information technology, or the understanding of psycho-physiological aspects of phenomena such as stress, fatigue, or insomnia. Psychology as used in the clinic may be well known, but it is just one branch of a much bigger subject.

## The aims and structure of this book

Our aim is to explain and illustrate why psychology is interesting, important, and useful today. As most psychologists are interested in people, examples will predominantly be drawn from human psychology. Nevertheless, the book starts from the assumption that the minimum condition for having a psychology, as opposed to being a plant or an amoeba, is the possession of a mental control system that enables the organism to operate both in and on the world. Once the brain and nervous system have evolved sufficiently to be used as a control centre, there are certain things it must be able to do: pick up information about the world outside itself, keep track of that information, store it for later use, and use it to organize its behaviour so as, crudely speaking, to get more of what it wants and less of what it does not want. Different organisms do these things in different ways (for example, they have different kinds of sense organs), and yet some of the processes involved are similar across species (for example, some types of learning, and some expressions of emotion). One of the central concerns of psychologists is to find out how these things come about. So Chapters 2–5 will focus on four of the most important questions that psychologists ask: What gets into the mind? What stays in the mind? How do we use what is in the mind? and Why do we do what we do? They aim to show how psychologists find out about the processes involved in perception and attention (Chapter 2), in learning and memory (Chapter 3), in thinking, reasoning, and communicating (Chapter 4), and in motivation and emotion (Chapter 5). These chapters explain the ways in which these processes work for us and they focus on generalities: the commonalities between people. They aim to describe our 'mental furniture', by looking at some of the hypotheses psychologists have made and a few of the models they have constructed to explain their observations.

Psychologists are also interested in the differences between people and in the determinants of their obvious variety. If we are going to understand people better we need to disentangle general influences from individual ones. If there were only general patterns and rules, and we all had the same mental furniture then all people would be psychologically identical, which of course they are not. So how do we explain how they come to be the way they are, and how do we understand their differences, their difficulties, and their interactions? Chapter 6 asks: Is there a set pattern of human development? Chapter 7 looks at individual differences and asks: Can we categorize people? Chapter 8 asks: What happens when things go wrong? and focuses on abnormal psychology, and Chapter 9 asks: How do we influence each other? and describes social psychology. Finally, in Chapter 10 we ask: What is psychology for?, we describe the practical uses to which psychology has been put, and offer some speculations about the types of advance that might be expected in the future.

# Chapter 2

# What gets into our minds?
# Perception

Look steadily at the drawing in Figure 3. This picture of a *Necker cube* is made up entirely of black lines in two-dimensional space, but what you *perceive* is a three-dimensional cube. Looking for some time at this cube produces an apparent reversal, so that the face that was in front becomes the back face of a cube facing the other way. These representations alternate even if you try not to let them do so. What you are seeing is the brain at work as it attempts to make sense of an ambiguous drawing, unable to settle for one interpretation or the other. It seems that perception is not just a matter of passively picking up information from the senses, but the product of an active construction process that involves combining input from sensory signals with other information.

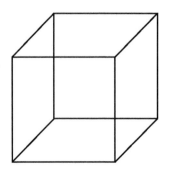

3. Necker cube

Even more confusing is the drawing of the devil's tuning fork (Figure 4) which misleads us by using standard cues for depth perception. Alternately we see, or cannot see, a three-dimensional representation of a three-pronged fork. Similar phenomena can be demonstrated using other senses. If you repeat the word 'say' to yourself quickly and steadily you will alternately hear 'say say say…' and 'ace ace ace…'. The point is the same: the brain works on the information received and makes hypotheses about reality without our conscious direction, so that what we are ultimately aware of is the product of *sensory stimulation* and activity in the brain which results in *interpretation.* If we are driving in thick fog, or trying to read in the dark, then the guesswork becomes obvious: 'Is this our turning or a drive-way?'; 'Does it say "head" or "dead"?' Sensory processes partly determine what gets into our minds, but we can already see that other hidden and complex processes also contribute to what we perceive.

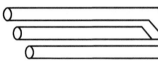

**4. The devil's tuning fork**

We generally assume that the world is as we see it and that others see it the same way—that our senses reflect an objective and shared reality. We assume that our senses represent the world in which we live as accurately as a mirror reflects the face that peers into it, or as a camera creates a snapshot of a particular instant, frozen in time. Of course if our senses did not provide us with generally accurate information we could not rely on them as we do, but nevertheless psychologists have found that these assumptions about perception are misleading. Picking up information about our worlds is not a passive, reflective process, but a complex, active one in which the senses and the brain work together, helping us to construct a *perception* (or illusion) of reality. We do not just see patterns of light, dark, and colour—we organize these patterns so that we see objects that have meaning for us. We can name or recognize them, and identify them as entirely new or similar to other objects. As we shall see throughout this book, psychological research has revealed some fascinating—and surprising—things, of which we may be unaware, that are going on in our minds. Studying these hidden processes has become an interdisciplinary matter with developments in the cognitive sciences, and especially in computational neuroscience, which is the study of brain function in terms of the information processing properties of the structures that make up the nervous system. This helps to shed light on the mechanisms by which we perceive and understand the vast array of information that impacts on our senses.

Most psychological research into perception has concentrated on visual perception because vision is our best developed sense: about half the *cortex* (the convoluted grey matter in the brain) is related to vision. Visual examples can also be illustrated, so they will predominate in this chapter.

## Perceiving the real world

The first stage of perception involves detecting the signal that something is out there. The human eye can detect only a minute fraction, less than 1 per cent, of all electromagnetic energy—the visible spectrum. Bees and butterflies can see ultraviolet rays, and some snakes can 'see' the radiant heat emitted by their prey sufficiently precisely to be able to target vulnerable parts of the body when they strike. So what we know about reality is limited by the capabilities of our sense organs. Within those limitations, our sensitivity is remarkable: on a clear dark night, we could theoretically see a single candle flame 30 miles away. When we detect a signal such as a light, our sensory receptors convert one form of energy into another, so information about the light is transmitted as a pattern of neural impulses. The raw material of perception for all the senses consists of neural impulses which are channelled to differently specialized parts of the brain. For the impulses to be interpreted as seeing a candle flame, they have to reach the visual cortex, and the pattern and rate of firing in activated cells and lack of firing in inhibited cells has both to be distinguished from the background level of cellular activity (or *neural noise*), and decoded. Interestingly, the ability to detect a signal accurately is far more variable than would be expected from knowledge about sensory systems alone, and is influenced by many other factors: some are obvious, like attention, others less obvious, involving our expectations, motivations, or inclinations, such as a tendency to say 'yes' or 'no' when uncertain. If you are listening to the radio while waiting for an important phone call, you may think you heard it ring when it did not, whereas if you are engrossed in the radio programme and not expecting a call you may completely fail to hear it ring. Such differences in detecting signals have important practical implications, for example in designing effective warning systems in intensive care units or control panels for complex machines.

Theories constructed to explain these findings enable psychologists to make and to test predictions. *Signal detection theory* suggests that accurate perception is determined not just by sensory capacity but by a combination of sensory processes and decision processes. Decisions vary according to the degree of cautiousness required (or *response bias*) in use at the time. A laboratory technician scanning slides for cancerous cells responds to every anomaly and sorts out the 'false alarms' later, but a driver deciding when to overtake the car in front must get it right each time or risk a collision. Measures of sensitivity and of cautiousness can be calculated by counting 'hit rates' and 'false alarms', and applying relatively simple statistical procedures to predict when a signal (a cancerous cell or an oncoming car) will be accurately detected. These measures have many practical uses, for example in training people to monitor baggage screening devices at airports.

All senses respond better to changes in the environment than to a steady state, and receptors stop responding altogether, or *habituate*, when nothing changes, so you notice the noise of the fridge when it switches on but not later. In our busy lives one might suppose that rest from sensory stimulation would be a boon, but *sensory deprivation*—the absence of all sensory stimulation—can induce frightening and bizarre experiences including hallucinations in some people. The degree of distress experienced varies according to what people expect. The same applies if the senses are overloaded for a significant length of time such as at pop concerts or football matches. These can be exhausting as well as stimulating experiences.

## The process of perception

One of the most basic perceptual processes is distinguishing objects from their surroundings. Look at the Rubin's vase (Figure 5). You will see either a vase or two silhouettes, but not both at once. Seeing the vase makes the silhouettes disappear, but seeing the silhouettes turns the vase into background.

Another process enables us to perceive important things before less important ones, so in Figure 6 we see H before S even though they are equally visible. So the brain is determining what we 'see'

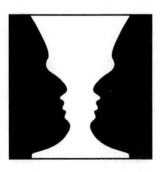

**5. Rubin's vase**

```
    S              S
    S              S
    S              S
    SSSSSSSSSS
    S              S
    S              S
    S              S
```

**6. Seeing H before S**

Psychology

as much as our eyes, and the processes involved seem to be designed to make sense of the input from our senses whenever possible. Psychologists hypothesize that there are several crucial steps in this process. Input from the senses (sensation) is fed into the brain which then uses knowledge it already has to construct a model of what is perceived: for example, 'That might be Jane'. The model tells us what to expect, and enables us to make predictions (in this case, about how Jane looks, walks, and sounds). Correct predictions confirm our expectations, and incorrect predictions provide new information that updates the internal model. This process goes on, constantly refining and updating our perceptions ('Oh—it *is* Jane—but she looks older now') as sensation and expectations interact to provide us with inferences about the world. These processes go on all the time, but we most easily become aware of them when faced with a perceptual difficulty such as an ambiguous figure or an illusion; or when meaningful signals are obscure or impermanent, as for Jane. Usually all of this happens without us knowing anything more about it than the resulting 'illusion' of being in direct contact with external reality.

One interesting, and debatable, idea about how the brain works is that it uses a form of Bayesian inference. Bayes's theorem was first published in 1763 and then ignored for more than a century. It provides a way of measuring, precisely, the value of a new piece of information in the context of current expectations or beliefs, and provides a computational basis for believing that perception is a product of the inferences we make when we combine sensory information with prior knowledge (previous knowledge about Jane with knowledge about subtle signs of ageing).

This model assumes that what we perceive depends on what we already know. Three sources of knowledge may be involved, together or separately. Learning: we learn fast from infancy on; knowledge that is biologically 'hard wired' into the brain by millions of years of evolution and may therefore be innate; and an innate predisposition to learn about particular sorts of things. Babies who are only a few days old prefer to look at faces rather than other similarly complex stimuli, and a specialized part of the brain (the fusiform face area) seems to be pre-programmed to process faces. Neural activity in this area can be detected when a face is expected but has not yet appeared in our visual field, and also when we imagine seeing a face. Then all three processes could be involved. Now look at the picture of the two dominos in Figure 7. You will see five convex and one concave spot in the top domino, while the bottom domino has only two convex spots. Turn the page upside down and the convex and concave spots reverse. The main hypothesis in this case has an evolutionary basis. Over millions of years we have developed a predisposition to learn that the source of light (the sun) comes from above, so convex objects will be light at the top and dark at the bottom, and for concave ones it will be the other way round. This knowledge, or rule, determines what we perceive. Turn the page sideways and neither of these interpretations dominates.

Making sense of what we perceive happens so naturally and effortlessly that it is hard to believe it is a substantial achievement. Computers can be programmed to play chess, but programming them to match even relatively rudimentary perceptual skills, such as turning the spoken word into the written form, is far harder. Brain imaging studies show that some cells respond most to lines having a specific orientation or length, and others may detect simple shapes or surfaces. Are we born with such specialized detectors, or do they

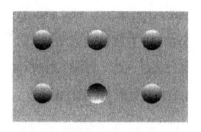

**7. The domino illusion**

develop later? Individuals who were born blind but regain their
sight as adults (for example, following the surgical removal of
congenital cataracts) find visual perception extremely difficult, and
continue to make visual errors. Processes that for others have
become automatic for them still involve guesswork, and integrating
visual information with information from other senses remains
effortful. Understanding the process of perception is easier if you
focus on one of the senses at a time, but most of the time the brain
has to deal with simultaneous input from the different sensory
modalities (sight and sound; sight, touch, smell, and taste, and so
on). The different sources of information have to be integrated if
they are to provide us with a coherent representation of the world
that corresponds to reality. These sources include sensations from
the body as well as information from the sense organs, which tells
us that bodily feelings and emotional states also play an important
part in the process of perception. Indeed, we may immediately
know whether we like—or dislike—the sound that we hear or the

person that we see coming, as the brain routinely makes affective predictions. Even before recognizing Jane we may feel a sense of warmth—or dread—as she approaches. In fact we can use any source of previous knowledge to generate predictions about what we perceive, including semantic knowledge, for example about the visible signs of ageing. The brain activity underlying perception, possibly using Bayesian inference, thus allows us to integrate information from the different sense organs, from internal body states, and from knowledge about the world, into the process of perception.

## Paying attention: making use of a limited capacity system

Perception involves more than the acquisition of discriminatory skills. It also involves forming hypotheses, generating predictions, and making corrections as we go along. It involves selection, and making decisions about what to focus on from amongst the many things that demand our attention. Our brains are limited capacity systems, and to make the best use of them it helps to direct our attention appropriately. If you audio-record a noisy party you would most likely hear something resembling a confused babble. But if you start talking—or paying attention—to someone at the party, your conversation will stand out against the background noise and you may not even know whether the person behind you was talking in French or English. Yet if someone mentions your name, without even raising their voice, you will be highly likely to notice it. Normally, we focus as we wish by filtering out what does not matter to us at the time, on the basis of *low level information*, such as the voice of the speaker or direction from which the voice comes.

Noticing our own name is a puzzling exception to this rule, and several explanations have been suggested for how the filter system works. We must know something about those things we ignore or

### Box 3 Subliminal perception: a means of self-protection?

Two spots of light are shown on a screen, and in one of them a word is written so faintly that it cannot be consciously perceived. Subjects judge the brightness of the spots as dimmer when there is an emotionally unpleasant word hidden in the light than when the word is pleasant or neutral. This has been called *perceptual defence* because it potentially can protect us from unpleasant stimuli.

we would not know that we wanted to ignore them. Perceiving something without realizing that we have done so has been called *subliminal perception* (Box 3). Laboratory studies have shown that our attentional processes can work so fast and efficiently that they can protect us from consciously noticing things that might upset us, such as obscene or disturbing words.

Paying attention is one way in which we select what gets into our minds—but we do not have to pay attention to only one thing at a time. In fact, divided attention is the norm. We can divide our attention most easily between information coming to us through different channels—which is why I can keep an eye on the children, while replying to an email and listening to the radio. I can even worry about the letter from the bank manager at the same time, but there are limits to this versatility. Air traffic controllers were once trained to do many things simultaneously: watch a radar screen, talk to pilots, track different flight paths, and read messages handed to them on paper. Provided the flow of traffic was manageable they could divide their attention in all these ways at once. However, during the development of safety systems, simulated tests of their capacity showed that if the flow of information was too great, or if they were tired, their responses became disorganized and even quite bizarre: standing up and pointing out directions to pilots thousands of feet up in the air and many miles away, or shouting loudly to get the information across.

It will be no surprise to learn that attention is a sensitive process. Many factors have been found to interfere with it, such as similarity between stimuli, difficulty of the task, lack of skill or practice, distress or worry, preoccupation or absent-mindedness, drugs, boredom, and sensory habituation. One reason why it is safer to use railways to transport people through a long underground tunnel, such as the one under the Channel between France and England, is that driving would be too risky. Without sufficient sensory variety perceptual systems habituate and attention wanders. We adapt, or habituate, to stimuli that do not change, and orient towards something new. So lying quite still in the bath I will not notice the gradual temperature change until I move about.

What we actually perceive, in combining perception and attention, is thus influenced by internal factors such as emotions and bodily states as well as by external factors. People who fear social rejection more readily notice signs of unfriendliness than of friendliness, such as negative facial expressions, and hungry people judge pictures of food as more brightly coloured than pictures of other things. These findings confirm that so much of perception goes on outside awareness that we cannot be sure that there is a good match between what we perceive and reality, or between what we perceive and what others perceive. Psychologists have suggested that two kinds of processing are involved.

- *Bottom-up processing* starts when we see something out in the real world which triggers a chain of activity in the brain. This tends to prevail when viewing conditions are good.

- *Top-down processing* reflects the contribution of conceptually driven, central processes. Even when reacting to light or sound waves each of us brings past experience (and attention) to the task, and if the viewing conditions are poor, or our expectations are strong, we will rely more on internal and less on external information.

Glance at the triangle in Figure 8 to see what it says. Did you notice the error? Most people do not do so at first, as their expectations about the well known phrase (top–down processing) interfere with accurate (bottom–up) perception. Occupying people with an attention-demanding task (counting the number of passes made by basketball players for example) has a similar effect. When doing this, most observers fail to notice anything else: even when a man dressed as a gorilla walks in full view behind the jugglers. In both cases the Bayesian brain is using prior knowledge to make predictions which then influence what is perceived, so we see what we expect to see, and we ignore what we do not expect to see.

**8. Paris in the spring**

## Learning from perceptual impairment: the man who mistook his wife for a hat

The complexities of perception mean that it can go wrong in many different ways. In *The Man Who Mistook His Wife for a Hat* Oliver Sacks describes what happens when more complex, interpretive perceptual abilities are seriously impaired. His patient was a talented musician, with no deterioration in his musical or other mental abilities. He was aware that he made mistakes, particularly in recognizing people, but not otherwise aware that anything much was wrong. He could converse normally, but no longer recognized his students, and confused inanimate objects (such as his shoe) with animate ones (his foot). At the end of an interview with Dr Sacks he looked for his hat, but instead reached for, and tried to lift off, his wife's head. He could not recognize the emotional expressions or the gender of people seen on TV, and could not identify members of his family from their photographs, even though he could do so by their voices. Sacks reports that 'visually he was lost in a world of lifeless abstractions'. He could see the world as a computer construes it, by means of key features and schematic relationships, so that when asked to identify a glove he described it as 'a container of some sort' and as 'a continuous surface infolded on itself [which] appears to have five outpouchings...' (p. 13). This severe perceptual impairment affected visual recognition more than other things: as if he could see without understanding or interpreting what he saw. Bereft of the interpretive aspect of perception, he came to a complete stop if he had to rely on visual information alone, but was able to keep going by humming to himself—by living in the musical, auditory world for which he was especially skilled. Although he could make hypotheses (about his wife's head or the glove)—as indeed we do when looking at the Necker cube (Figure 3)—he could not make judgements about those things. Studying carefully the selective impairment of high-level perceptual functions provides clues that help us to understand many things: the part that those functions play, not only in perception but in helping us to live in the real world; which functions are separately coded in the brain and where the organization of those functions is located.

So perception is the end product of complex processes, many of which take place out of awareness. Psychologists have now learned so much about perception that they can simulate a visual environment sufficiently accurately for trainee surgeons to use *'virtual reality'* to practise doing complex operations. Virtual reality creates the illusion of three-dimensional space, so that it becomes possible on a computer to reach round something or pass through 'solid' objects. Perceptual systems are able to learn and adapt quickly—however, being able to do this is a mixed blessing. Surgeons who have practised like this until their use of standard perceptual cues for moving around safely in three-dimensional space has readjusted are especially prone to car accidents afterwards.

This introduction to the field of perception only starts to answer questions about what gets into the mind. The subject covers many more fascinating topics ranging from ideas about perceptual development to debates about the degree to which the processes involved in perception are automatic or can be intentionally controlled. The aim has been to illustrate the point that reality as we know it is partly an individual, human construction. Each of us makes it up as we go along, and psychologists help us to understand many of the conditions which determine how we do this. If we know something about what gets into the mind, we can go on to ask how much of it stays there, becoming the basis for what we learn and remember.

# Chapter 3
# What stays in the mind? Learning and memory

When you learn something it makes a difference. There is something you can do that you could not do before, like play the piano, or there is something that you now know that you did not know before, like what 'empirical' means. When something stays in the mind, we assume it is stored somewhere, and we call this storage system 'memory'. The system does not work perfectly: we sometimes have to 'rack our brains' or 'search our memories', but perhaps the most common preconception about what stays in the mind is that there is a place where it is all stored. Sometimes we cannot find what we want, but it is probably there somewhere if only we knew where to look. Psychologists' discoveries about learning and memory show that the two processes are interdependent but that the analogy of the repository is not accurate.

About memory, William James asked in 1890:

> why should this absolute god-given Faculty retain so much better
> the events of yesterday than those of last year, and, best of all, those
> of an hour ago? Why, again, in old age should its grasp of
> childhood's events seem firmest? Why should repeating an
> experience strengthen our recollection of it? Why should drugs,
> fevers, asphyxia, and excitement resuscitate things long since
> forgotten? ... such peculiarities seem quite fantastic; and might, for
> aught we can see a priori, be the precise opposites of what they are.

Evidently, then, *the faculty does not exist absolutely, but works under conditions*; and *the quest of the conditions* becomes the psychologist's most interesting task. (*Principles of Psychology*, i. 3)

Understanding what stays in the mind is still a challenge. First, it is important to recognize that learning and memory are two sides of the same coin: we know that people (and animals) have learned something when they show or tell us what they remember. Some change has registered in their brains, and cognitive scientists, including psychologists, have discovered much about the processes involved in creating and maintaining this change. Box 4 provides an example with important implications for both learning and memory, and clearly the research raises questions as well as answering them.

This kind of research was made possible by the development of *in vivo* neuroimaging techniques, which are able to visualize the structure and workings of the living human brain. During the

### Box 4  Navigating and the brain

The brains of London taxi drivers change as they become expert navigators. The volume of grey matter in the mid-posterior hippocampus increases, and in the anterior hippocampus it decreases. The more years of experience the greater these changes. No such changes are found in the brains of London bus drivers, matched in many ways, including for driving experience and level of stress, but who follow predetermined routes rather than developing the navigational expertise of taxi drivers. However there is also a cost: the decreases in grey matter are associated with difficulty in acquiring new visuo-spatial memories.

Maguire, Woollett, and Spiers (2006); Woollett and Maguire (2011).

research described in Box 4 MRI scanners measured volumetric differences in the hippocampus, which plays a crucial part in the formation of new memories. These and subsequent results can tell us about the plasticity of the brain, about the functions of specific parts of the brain and how they operate, about structural pathways which link different parts of the brain, about which functions are separately organized, and how different functions interact. Similarly, such studies can have implications for rehabilitation, for example in memory-impaired patients.

## Learning: making the connections that last

We tend to assume that the ability to learn is determined by such things as how clever you are, whether you pay attention, and whether you persist when the going gets tough. But it turns out that there are different kinds of learning, many of which involve no conscious effort or formal instruction. We are learning all the time, throughout our lives, even if we are not attempting to do so, and some of the ways in which we learn are similar to the ways in which other animals learn, despite our greater capacity. Learning is triggered in a number of different ways. Environments vary so enormously that adaptation is essential. Humans and other animals adapt well because they are predisposed to learn, and because they respond particularly strongly to certain types of events: *contingencies*—what goes together with what—and *discrepancies*—differences from the norm.

Learning about contingencies allows one to make things happen: turn the tap and the water (usually) runs. By learning how to turn the tap on and off we learn how to control the flow of water. Tiny babies repeatedly explore contingencies: waving their arms about, they hit something that makes a noise and do this over and over again, until they can control the noise they make. This apparent fascination with contingencies is an important basis for other types of learning such as skill learning. Once you have mastered a skill you can do it without thinking and turn your attention to something else: when once you can read words effortlessly you can think about their meaning. If you can play the tune automatically you can think about how to interpret the music.

Knowing what to expect makes discrepancies fascinating—provided they are not too radical. Small changes in a child's world (a new type of food, sleeping somewhere new) invite exploration and help the child to learn, but if everything is suddenly disrupted then the child becomes anxious. In the same way, different ways of singing the song (playing the game) become interesting once you know its basic pattern. This ability to learn by making distinctions is lasting and fundamental. Older people are better at new learning when they already have relevant stored knowledge and are therefore noticing and adjusting to discrepancies, but they are worse at learning something completely new. We remain responsive to contingencies and discrepancies throughout our lives, and both processes are involved in the two kinds of associative learning described next.

## Associative learning

Perhaps the most basic of the many different kinds of learning is *association learning* or *conditioning*, of which there are two types: classical and instrumental (or operant) conditioning. *Classical conditioning* was first explored and understood by Pavlov, working with dogs in the 1920s. Having found a way of measuring their salivation in response to food he noticed that the dogs started to salivate before they were given the food. The reflexive, or *unconditioned response*, of salivation was triggered by things associated with the food, like the sight of the bowl, the person who brought the food, or the sound of the bell that was paired with the food (rung as the food appeared). Pavlov showed that virtually any stimulus could become a *conditioned stimulus* for salivation—the sound of a metronome, a triangle drawn on a large card, and even an electric shock, and he concluded that learning takes place when a previously neutral stimulus (a bell) is associated with an *unconditioned stimulus* (something to which we naturally respond, such as food). Classical conditioning has been minutely studied, so we know how conditioned responses die away or generalize to similar things; how emotions can be conditioned (a child's fear of the waves) and counter-conditioned (by holding a parent's hand while paddling), and new associations can be made quite dramatically in 'one-trial learning'—as when you happen to become ill after eating a novel food and you never want to eat it again.

*Instrumental conditioning*, first investigated by B. F. Skinner, explains the powerful part played by *reinforcement* in learning. The main idea is that if an action is followed by a pleasant effect (a reward) it will be repeated—whether performed by a man or a rat. If pressing a lever brings with it a food pellet, a rat will learn to press the lever. The hungrier it is the faster it will learn, and the strength of its response can be precisely predicted by the rate at which the food pellets are dispensed. The rat will 'work' hardest if the pellets arrive intermittently and unpredictably (which is how fruit machines—or capricious lovers—keep us hooked), and least hard if the pellets arrive after the same amount of time whatever the rat does. Hence, people paid at a constant rate for doing boring, repetitive work quickly lose motivation in comparison to those paid piece-rate. Using the principles of reinforcement, extraordinary feats of learning have been demonstrated, such as teaching pigeons to 'play' table tennis with their beaks by *shaping* their behaviour gradually in the right direction. (See Figure 9.)

Instrumental conditioning has many practical applications. If you want a response to continue after it has been learned, such as getting a child to tidy up, you should reward it intermittently, not continuously. If you occasionally reward a behaviour you want to decrease (for example, angry outbursts or tantrums) you will strengthen the behaviour by mistake. If a reward arrives too late, it will be far less effective (for example, thanking an employee a week after you received their report rather than immediately). Reinforcement thus provides the fuel for the learning machine, which works equally well whether the reinforcement is positive,

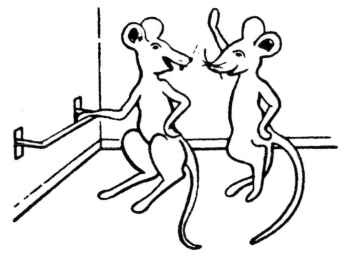

9. 'Boy, do we have this guy conditioned. Every time I press the bar down he drops a pellet in.' Operant conditioning from another point of view

providing something pleasant, or negative, taking away something unpleasant (for example, if you miss a show you wanted to see, you learn to plan ahead).

Skinner had strong views about punishment, which is easy to confuse with, but very different from, negative reinforcement. He believed that it was an ineffective way of helping people to learn because it is painful but uninformative. It works by discouraging a particular kind of behaviour without suggesting what to do instead. In fact, punishment raises complex issues. It can be effective, for example in reducing self-injurious behaviour such as head banging, and it can be administered in mild but effective ways (a spray of water in the face, or *time-out* from the situation). But its effects may be temporary, or only effective in specific circumstances (not smoking in front of parents but continuing to do so with friends). Punishment is not often easy to deliver immediately, it conveys little information, and may be unintentionally rewarding—a teacher's reprimand to one naughty pupil may attract reinforcing kinds of attention from others in the class.

Principles of instrumental learning have been used to develop effective *behaviour modification* techniques in many settings such as schools, hospitals, and prisons. They have been applied usefully to toilet training but also in attempts to achieve inappropriate political control. One reason why this sort of abuse of power may not be the risk that was once feared is that there is room, psychologically speaking, for an element of determinism and for an element of free will in the sequence of events that lead up to a person's actions. Association learning is not the only possibility. If you notice that an advertiser is associating a new car with sexual potency, you can decide to take it or leave it on more rational grounds. If someone is nice to you for non-genuine motives you may not find the contact rewarding and fail to warm to them. Clearly, we can use other types of learning, and other cognitive abilities as well.

## Complex learning

Complex learning uses other cognitive processes as well as those involved in associative learning. For example observation, imitation, and acceptance of social norms may all play a part, as do expectations based on prior beliefs. An example of *observational learning* is shown in Box 5.

The ability to use prior knowledge is demonstrated by *latent learning*. If you have looked at a map of a new city, or have travelled through it as a passenger, you will learn your way around it faster than someone who is completely new to it, and your learning advantage can be accurately measured. *Insight learning* also demonstrates an ability to draw on what is already represented in the mind. This occurs when you suddenly see the solution to a problem: how to fix the broken lamp. The understanding sometimes comes in a flash, and it is not clear whether it is purely

**Box 5 Observational learning: when others set a bad example**

Young children watched someone playing with some toys, in real life, on film, or as shown in a cartoon, where sometimes the person hit one of the dolls.

The children were then taken to the same playroom—some being allowed to play with the toys and some being frustrated by the experimenter removing the toy they were playing with.

The frustrated children tended to imitate the aggressive behaviour they had observed—and, in addition, they copied real life models more closely than filmed or cartoon models.

Further studies show that children are more likely to imitate models similar to themselves (children of the same age and sex) and people they admire.

Bandura and Walters (1963).

the result of previous learning or whether it involves creativity, mentally combining old responses in new ways, as we do when we combine words in new ways so as to express our own ideas.

Cognitive theories of learning have moved away from the associationist view and tried to explain the influences of other processes, such as attention, imagination, thinking, and feeling. As soon as we start to look at the ways in which new learning interacts with what is already in the mind the distinction between learning and memory becomes blurred. Memory, like perception, is an active process and not just a tape recording of all that you have learned. The more use you make of the material you learn (reading a French newspaper, speaking and writing to a French friend, watching French films, revising your grammar), the more you will remember. Material that is passively imbibed is easily forgotten and the differences that learning makes to what stays in the mind can be more fully understood by exploring the determinants of what we remember—by finding out how our memory works.

## Memory: shadows, reflections, or reconstructions?

Big claims have been made for memory, for example that it defines who we are, shapes the way we behave, and provides the basis for language, art, science, and culture. So how does it work? First we will look at a selection of research findings.

As early as 1932 Sir Frederic Bartlett showed that remembering is not just a question of making an accurate record of the information we receive, but involves fitting the new information into what is already there and creating a narrative that makes sense (see Box 6).

Bartlett argued that the process of retrieval involves reconstruction, which is influenced by the frameworks that people already have in

### Box 6  'The War of the Ghosts'

Bartlett read to a group of people an American Indian legend in which a man watches a battle involving ghosts, recounts what he has seen to some other people, and then suddenly succumbs to a wound received from a ghost. People made sense of the unfamiliar material by fitting it into their own pre-existing ideas and cultural expectations. For example, 'something black came out of his mouth' was reproduced as 'escaping breath' or 'foamed at the mouth'; or the people in the story were assumed to be members of a clan called 'The Ghosts'. The changes they made when remembering the story fitted with their reactions and emotions when first hearing it, and as one subject said, 'I wrote out the story mainly by following my own images'.

Bartlett (1932).

their heads. So memory, just like perception, is both selective and interpretive. It involves construction as well as reconstruction.

We are able to recall the meaning of events far more accurately than their details, and the meaning we give to them influences the details we remember. At the time of the Watergate trials, the psychologist Ulric Neisser compared tape recordings of conversations held in the White House with reports of these conversations from one of the witnesses, John Deane, who had an exceptionally good memory. He found that the meaning of Deane's memories was accurate but that the details, including some especially 'memorable' phrases, were not. Deane was right about what happened, but wrong about the words used and the order in which topics were discussed.

At particularly important or emotional moments, details tend to get better 'fixed' in our memories. However, even then the details remembered by two people present at the same event may be strikingly different. If I faced the blue sea and my husband faced the dark forest when we decided to marry each other, 20 years later we can argue about where we were at the time, and accuse each other of forgetting important shared memories, because one of us remembers the darkness and the other remembers the light. 'The past... is always an argument between counterclaimants' (Cormac McCarthy, *The Crossing*, p. 411).

How we decide between counterclaimants is still an important issue. It is possible that people brought up in painful and distressing circumstances, in which they felt neglected or victimized, later remember accurately the meaning to them of the events in their childhoods, but are incorrect about the details. This could explain some instances of *false memory syndrome* in which people are said to 'recover memories', for example of being abused as children, that turn out not to be accurate. It is also possible that the details of unusual or intense experiences *are* accurately remembered. The mistake is to believe that remembering details and believing that those details are accurate prove that the memories are correct.

38

Even when we do remember details accurately, the details we remember are not fixed in our memories, but remain changeable. If I witnessed an accident at a junction and am later questioned about details of what happened, such as whether the car stopped before or after the tree, I am likely to insert a tree into my memory even if there was no tree. Once that tree has been inserted it seems to become part of the original memory, so that I can no longer tell the difference between my 'real' memory and what I remember remembering later. So memories once told can be changed by the telling (which may explain how we sometimes come to believe our own lies), and questions asked of witnesses in court ('did you see *a* broken head lamp' vs. 'did you see *the* broken head lamp') affect what is recalled without people knowing that this has happened.

People often wish for perfect, or photographic, memory. However, being unable to forget may have its disadvantages (Box 7), and the creative, rather inaccurate, system of remembering and forgetting that we have may be well adapted for our purposes.

### Box 7 The mind of a mnemonist

A man was able to remember huge series of numbers or words after seeing them for only a few seconds—he could repeat them forwards or backwards even after a gap of 15 years. This man's memory appeared to work by making the information he received meaningful. He associated each part of it with visual and other sensory images, making the elements unique and 'unforgettable'. But these images subsequently interfered so much with concentration that he could no longer perform simple activities including holding conversations, and became unable to function in his profession as a journalist. The problem was that new information, such as the words he heard others speak, set off an uncontrollable train of distracting associations.

Alexander Luria (1968).

How do models of memory account for findings as diverse as these? And what do they tell us about the function of memory? Cognitive neuroscience has made strides in answering these questions, and provides a good example of the benefits of collaboration between psychologists and other scientists. The three different stages of memory, encoding, storage, and retrieval, are now known to be associated with activity in different parts of the brain. *Sensory memory* holds a large amount of information but only for about a second. Paying attention to the content of sensory memory transfers incoming information to *working memory*, and information that is not transferred is quickly lost and cannot be retrieved, just as lights fade and sounds die away. Working memory has a limited capacity. Most people can remember around seven items (or more precisely 7 +/− 2) by verbally rehearsing them. Active rehearsal (muttering a phone number to yourself, or keeping two numbers in mind so as to add them together) keeps information in working memory, and we can increase the amount remembered by chunking the material using information in *long-term memory* to recode it into larger, meaningful units, so the limit may be seven letters, seven words, or seven lines of a song (the so-called 'magical number seven'). The process by which memories are encoded into long-term memory and stabilized, *consolidation*, happens in two ways. *Synaptic consolidation*, effected in hippocampal regions of the brain, occurs within the first few hours of learning and *systemic consolidation* involves transfer of information to the cortex, and occurs over a period of time varying between weeks and years.

Functional brain imaging studies have revealed that the activity of various brain regions changes over time after a new memory is acquired. The hippocampus plays a crucial part in this process. It is known to be important for learning new information and for memory consolidation, and to have input and output channels that link it to different parts of the brain. Bilateral damage to the hippocampus makes it impossible to lay down new episodic (event) memories, or consciously to remember experiences

40

preceding the damage by as much as a couple of years. Motor skills are usually retained, and procedural memories (how to ride a bike) can still be laid down while memories for events earlier than this remain unaffected. However we are still some way from understanding exactly how complex memories are stored, and how we succeed—or fail—in retrieving them when we wish to. It may sound as if information in long-term memory is not lost when we forget: it has just become difficult to access. This suggests that forgetting occurs because similar memories become confused and interfere with each other when we try to recall them. So, unless we have the mind of a mnemonist, one birthday party becomes confused with another and what we remember in the end is something about the significance of birthdays rather than exactly what happened when we were 5 or 10 or 15. General meanings are more important than details unless something marks those details for us (a 21st birthday or a surprise party).

So how can you establish what really happened? Or do we even need to? Evolutionary considerations may help to explain why memory works as we know (so far) that it does. Our memory systems did not evolve because we need to catalogue the items and events in the world but rather because we need to survive in a changing world. There are things we need to remember, like how to find the way home or correct our mistakes or recognize danger, and things we do not need to remember, like precise details of our past. We need to select, interpret, and integrate one thing with another: to make use of incoming information and of what we learn, and memory is an activity that helps us to do these things.

Learning and memory, like the perceptual system described in Chapter 2, are active systems that employ organizing principles. Information stays in the mind more easily if, for example, it is *relevant*, *distinctive* in some way, has been *elaborated upon* or worked with, and processed meaningfully as opposed to superficially. Organizing information we want to remember confers an advantage when it comes to remembering it (thinking of 'picnic food', or 'school lunches' as you walk round the supermarket). Some general principles of organization have been discovered, but at the same time each of us develops a personal organizational system based on past experience. So we encode or organize incoming information differently, and have different priorities or interests when retrieving it. This helps us to adapt in the present: to avoid situations that trouble us and to seek out the kind of work that feels satisfying. But it also means that our memories are not just 'snapshots' of the past. Just as we saw that perceiving and attending to the outside world involves constructing a view of reality, so we now see that learning and memory are also active, constructive processes. Furthermore, the accuracy of our memories may be irrelevant for many purposes. In order to make the best use of what stays in the mind, it may be more important to remember meanings—and to use these as we think, reason, and communicate—than to remember precisely what happened.

# Chapter 4

# How do we use what is in the mind? Thinking, reasoning, and communicating

Behaving thoughtlessly, not stopping to think, being unreasonable or illogical, and being unable to explain our reasons for doing something are failings to which everyone is susceptible. The assumption is that when we do these things we are *failing*: we *should* think before we act, be thoughtful and reasonable, and be able to communicate clearly. However, psychologists have made some rather surprising discoveries about this type of behaviour and some of the more recent discoveries are outlined next. In 2002, Daniel Kahneman, described by the philosopher Steven Pinker as 'among the most influential psychologists in history', was awarded a Nobel prize—in economic sciences. Why should this prize be given to a psychologist? The answer is to be found in his work on thinking and reasoning. This work helped to define the new field of *behavioural economics* to which various governments in the Western world now pay close attention. For instance, in 2011 the UK government established a number of *behavioural insight teams* whose task is to apply specific psychological findings to the business of government. Behavioural economists study the effects of social, cognitive, and emotional factors on the economic decisions of individuals and institutions, and these of course are subject to the same influences as other judgements and decisions that we make, and are also central subjects for psychologists.

In Chapters 2 and 3 it was argued that what gets into the mind and what stays there subsequently is not solely determined by the nature of objective reality, but also by the processes involved in perception learning and remembering. If we can make sense of what we perceive, recall information when it is needed, and use it when we think, reason, and communicate, then we can make plans, have ideas, solve problems, imagine more or less fantastic possibilities, and tell others all about it.

## Thinking: the costs and the benefits

Thinking uses up energy, and this energy and our use of it has evolved until it is now super-efficient. The human brain runs on about a quarter of the power of an 80–100 watt bulb, controlling everything we do: our senses, movements, internal states such as digestion, and our thinking. The pressure has been to evolve systems that only invest in energy use when there is something to be gained—hence perhaps the relevance to economics. One of Kahneman's most important suggestions is that we have evolved two systems of thinking which are distinguished by their use of energy: a fast one that costs us little, and a slow one that costs much more. These two systems also have different benefits.

*System 1* is the fast, intuitive, and automatic one. The benefit is that it takes minimal effort; the cost is that it means we take short-cuts and make mistakes. Much of the time it works well: complete the sentence 'bread and..'; add these numbers $2 + 2 = \ldots$; decide when to overtake the car in front; recognize at a glance that someone is angry. These tasks take little effort or voluntary control, as we can do them without thinking—once we have acquired some linguistic, mathematical, driving or social skills. System 1 helps us to make intuitive judgements—so we escape from danger without having to think about it—and it makes use of the information we have learned and collected in associative memory—so we can distinguish surprises from normal events and automatically use acquired skills. Although System 1 serves us well most of the time, it also means that we jump to conclusions, relying on rules of thumb or '*heuristics*', which introduce biases into our thinking and reasoning.

*System 2* is slow, deliberate, and effortful thinking. It brings with it benefits of conscious thinking and rationality, but has high energy costs. It requires attention, of which we have limited capacity. As we saw in Chapter 2, when our attention is fully occupied in counting the passes made by basketball players we are blind to the gorilla passing behind them. System 2 thinking: deciding which car to buy, filling in the tax return, explaining how to work the DVD player, etc., is tiring. It can also be moderately aversive, as our brains have evolved to maximize conservation of energy and conscious thinking demands application. The '*law of least effort*' operates throughout our thinking processes, and tells us that, if there are several ways of doing the same thing, people will gravitate towards the easiest one, which is why Kahneman described System 2 thinking as lazy. Paying attention helps us acquire and use our knowledge, but this comes at a cost—quite literally.

The division of labour between System 1 and System 2 is highly efficient. For example, System 1 runs automatically and generates intuitions or impressions and System 2 switches on when effort is needed. For example, I can easily guess whether I have been given the right change, but in order to check I have to stop and think. This division of labour can draw on culturally and personally relevant information also: for example, I immediately realize that my colleague is unwell and think about how to take the pressure off her during the meeting. System 2 is interrupted if attention is drawn away from it. Sometimes this is efficient: you lose the thread in the conversation when you hear the child yell (automatically alerted by System 1), at other times it is disruptive:

you lose track when irritated by the munching of the person next to you in the cinema.

To make efficient use of a short supply of energy we tend to rely on System 1 whenever possible, and this accounts for some common mistakes. The risk we run is illustrated by one of Kahneman's examples. Read the following simple puzzle and allow your intuition to come up quickly with an answer.

> A bat and a ball cost $1.10
> The bat costs one dollar more than the ball
> How much does the ball cost?

What number did you come up with? The quick and easy (System 1) answer is 10 cents. But this intuitive answer is wrong: it leaves the bat costing $1.00 which is only 90 cents more than the ball. Engage System 2 to work it out and you will discover the correct answer. As you can quickly tell, this uses more energy and—at least some—concentrated effort (solution in Box 13).

System 1 automatically makes use of associative links in the brain, including links to the body and to emotions, that subsequently influence our actions and feelings—again, in ways that we are unaware of, and therefore cannot prevent. Research on *priming* is revealing. For example, after being exposed to signs of money (floating dollar bills on a screensaver) people behaved differently: they became more independent, persevered longer with difficult problems, sat further away from others, and were less helpful (they picked up fewer of the pencils dropped by a clumsy research confederate). Exposed to words associated with old age in the USA (Florida, forgetful, bald) hidden in scrambled sentences and without mentioning age, young people subsequently walked more slowly down the hallway as they left the building. Even though they were completely unaware of noticing these words, seeing them influenced their actions and produced an *ideomotor effect*. This works the other way round as well: ask people to walk slowly

46

and they become faster at recognizing words associated with old age. Thinking about stabbing a colleague in the back leaves people more inclined to buy soap, disinfectant, or detergent rather than batteries, juice, or candy bars. As Kahneman puts it: 'feeling that one's soul is stained appears to trigger a desire to cleanse one's body'—the 'Lady Macbeth effect'. It even influences links to different parts of the body: if you ask someone to tell a lie to a stranger over the phone, later they prefer mouthwash over soap. Telling the lie by email shifts their preference to the soap. These findings support theories of *embodied cognition*, which suggest that almost all aspects of cognition depend on and make use of 'low-level' facilities such as the sensorimotor system and emotions, so are rooted in the body as well as the mind. The degree to which our behaviour is influenced by System 1, thinking that is effortless, automatic, and inaccessible to reflection, is particularly well illustrated by the experiment in Box 8.

Analysis of System 1 shows that our thinking is, and always will be, subject to influences that we cannot be aware of. Indeed, thinking consciously about some activities that have become automatic (running downstairs) is remarkably disruptive. Relegating them to the subconscious increases efficiency, allowing us to do them without thinking even at the cost of occasional absent-mindedness—putting the frozen peas in the bread bin, or driving home and forgetting to make a planned detour to the postbox on the way. It leaves spare thinking capacity for more important matters. The study of such *cognitive failures* (e.g. absent-mindedness) shows that they increase with stress, fatigue, or confusion, and can be reduced by 'stopping to think'.

Non-conscious mental activities demonstrably affect our thinking even though they remain outside awareness. Solutions to problems, or creative ideas, may pop into our heads apparently without previous thought, enabling us to see new ways forward: how to negotiate a deal or secure a broken window. More

## Box 8 Hidden influences on our behaviour

Near to an honesty box in which people placed coffee fund contributions, researchers at Newcastle University in the UK alternately displayed images of eyes and of flowers. Each image was displayed for a week at a time. During all the weeks in which eyes were displayed bigger contributions were made than in the weeks with flower images. Over the ten weeks of the study, contributions during the 'eyes weeks' were almost three times higher than those made in the 'flowers weeks'. It was suggested that 'the evolved psychology of co-operation is highly sensitive to subtle cues of being watched', and that the findings may have implications for how to provide effective nudges towards socially beneficial outcomes.

In this 'real world' field study, the honesty box was run by someone likely to be known to the participants, which might have influenced their behaviour. A follow-up study measuring the amount of litter left in a large cafeteria also found that people were less likely to litter in the presence of posters of eyes than of flowers, and that their behaviour was independent of whether the posters exhorted people to clear up or displayed unrelated messages. There appears to be good support for strong links between images of eyes, the sense of being observed, and the decision to engage in this type of cooperative behaviour.

Bateson, Nettle, and Roberts (2006); Ernest-Jones, Nettle, and Bateson (2011).

surprisingly, we can also make a decision to act without being aware of doing so. Olympic sprinters can take off in less than one-tenth of a second before they can consciously perceive the sound of the starting gun, and changes in brain activity can be identified before people are aware of their intention to move. Did they make the decision to move? Or not?

# Reasoning: using your head

One might suppose that reasoning using System 2 is more reliable—and allows us consciously to notice, or to ignore, information that could otherwise influence us unawares, such as the suggestion in advertisements that success comes with owning particular expensive products. We acquire the building blocks of rationality: we think with images and with words, we use concepts, create them, define them, recognize their clear or fuzzy boundaries, use them to define prototypes and to recognize stereotypes. We arm ourselves with skills needed to lead rational lives, such as methods of *deductive* or *inductive* reasoning. However, even these are demonstrably influenced by psychological processes. Deductive reasoning follows formal rules of logic, allowing us to draw conclusions which necessarily follow from the premises. From the two premises 'everyone with fair hair has blue eyes' and 'Sam has fair hair' we can validly draw the conclusion that 'Sam has blue eyes'. The conclusion will be false if either of the premises is false (as the first one clearly is), but the reasoning remains correct. But even if we succeed in reasoning logically, biases and mistakes creep in. For example, our thinking is biased towards reinforcing our current beliefs and away from accepting information that contradicts them. Research results showing that smoking causes cancer or that the performance of a group of skilled investors on the stock market remained at chance level were unwelcome to those selling cigarettes or stocks, and (initially) difficult for them to accept.

Inductive reasoning involves drawing conclusions that are probably true even though information yet to be discovered might show them to be false. It is commonly used in everyday life: 'Mary criticized what I said and dismissed my arguments out of hand'—'Therefore Mary is a critical person'. It often works well but is also subject to common biases: for example, seeking out information that confirms our conclusions (or suspicions) rather than going through the effortful process of looking for disconfirming information: in this case, that I make many mistakes rather than that Mary is always critical. As William James put it, 'a great many people think they are thinking when they are merely rearranging their prejudices'.

System 2 thinking, when the effort is put in, helps us to be rational. It enables us to work things out: to follow rules and to make deliberate comparisons, choices, and decisions. But it has limited capacity and needs to conserve energy. Its activities are determined by the workings as well as by the structure of our brains, and honed by our evolutionary history, with the result that we are averse to mental effort. So we engage System 1, employ effort-reducing heuristics, and remain subject to biases. One of the big debates, for instance in behavioural economics, has been about the degree to which we behave as rational beings, and many of the findings suggest that we do so far less than we suppose.

*Anchoring* is perhaps the best known, and most pervasive, cognitive bias that distorts our powers of reasoning. Kahneman and his colleague Tversky rigged a wheel of fortune, marked from 0 to 100, to stop only at numbers 10 or 65. After spinning the wheel, they asked participants in this experiment some completely unrelated questions such as 'What is your best guess of the percentage of African nations in the UN?'. Those who saw the number 10 guessed 25 per cent; those who saw number 65 guessed 45 per cent. They were all influenced by a completely irrelevant number, and their guesses were 'drawn' towards whichever anchor they had seen. When valuing a house, estate agents primed with a high, but irrelevant, anchor come up with a higher value than those primed with a low anchor—and a higher starting price can suggest a higher value, and bring in higher offers. This appears to be both a matter of suggestion (about value) and a consequence of failing to adjust sufficiently despite knowing about the bias (that the asking price could be inflated). If you ask people to nod or to shake their heads, as if they were saying yes or no, they adjust less (stay closer to the anchor offered) if they nod than if they shake.

The *availability* heuristic involves estimating the probability of a certain type of event on the basis of how easy it is to bring to mind relevant instances. The more readily available, the more likely it will seem to us to be. So when the printer does not work I check whether I turned it on, as my usual mistake springs readily to mind. The heuristic often brings with it problem-solving advantages that outweigh its disadvantages. The main disadvantage is that there are many determinants of availability—of what springs readily to mind—such as whether information has been accessed *recently*, is especially *vivid*, or *emotionally charged*, and all of these factors may be logically irrelevant. People who are frightened of flying tend to overestimate the likelihood of plane crashes, but they do so more dramatically if they have recently read about a crash. Some more of the biases that influence our thinking are listed in Box 9.

In most areas of life and much of the time, we are making judgements and decisions under conditions of uncertainty. We are thinking about what to do, or what will happen without knowing the answers. Will it rain? Can I afford a holiday? How am I doing at work? We have the ability to reason logically, and to avoid some obvious sources of irrationality, and we can save energy by switching into automatic modes without putting our lives at risk (driving on the motorway while having an interesting conversation). When faced with problems both systems have their uses.

Psychologists studying problem-solving have been particularly interested in the way it is influenced by past experience—by information stored in memory. It sounds obvious that, in general, we solve problems more easily as we accumulate experience. This is known as the *positive transfer effect*, and it helps to explain why adults solve problems more easily than children, and experts solve

## Box 9 Sources of some typical thinking errors

*Base-rate neglect*: Making a judgement about the probability of an outcome (that your business will succeed) while ignoring the general base rate (a 25 per cent success rate in this area).

*Framing*: Different ways of presenting the same information evoke different emotions (the glass is half full or half empty), and different decisions.

*Halo effect, or exaggerated emotional coherence*: Noticing one good (or bad) characteristic leads to the assumption that the rest are also good (or bad).

*Intensity matching*: Assuming that attributes that can be measured on a dimension are easily matched, e.g. Jim is as tall as he is clever.

*Loss aversion*: Losses loom larger to us than gains. We will work harder not to lose £500 than to win £500.

*Over confidence*: We overestimate the amount we know and underestimate the role of chance.

*Endowment effect*: The tendency to value something more highly when we own it than when someone else owns it.

them more easily than novices. Experts are better at solving a chess problem for instance, but both novices and experts benefit from a period of *incubation* during which they are not (consciously) thinking about the problem at all. Once a strategy for solving a problem has been identified, it may take skill to apply the strategy (rescuing the curdled mayonnaise), and reasoning skills are needed to evaluate progress. Experts are demonstrably better at recognizing patterns, retrieving relevant rules, and eliminating dead-end strategies. But experts can also fail to solve problems precisely because they use the same strategies and rules as they have used to solve previous problems. Developing a *mental set* prevents us having to reinvent the wheel each time but slows us up when faced with a new set of difficulties. It is remarkable how blind experts can become (see Box 10).

*Functional fixedness*, or thinking about objects only in terms of their functions, is another kind of mental set. An envelope is something to put a letter into rather than a container for sugar when you are having a picnic. Solving the sugar problem requires thinking about envelopes in new and creative ways. Creativity has been measured in various ways: for example, by testing the degree to which people think *divergently*, exploring ideas freely and generating many solutions, or *convergently*, following a set of steps which appear to converge on one correct solution to a problem. The more uses they can think of for common objects such as a house brick the more divergent or creative they are said to be. Creativity can be used in many ways: creative people are better than others at rationalizing their actions, and have been observed to cheat more too.

We know that creativity is present at an early age: that young children can use familiar concepts in new and imaginative ways, and that environments that foster independent thinking in a safe way increase creativity. Creativity is important in the arts, in science, in the kitchen, or in the office, and it may confer adaptive advantages by fostering the inventiveness needed in constantly changing conditions. It requires flexibility of thinking and an ability to step over boundaries (see Box 11), and, surprisingly to some people, it is only weakly correlated with intelligence. Characteristics such as nonconformity, confidence, curiosity, and persistence are at least as important as intelligence in determining creativity.

## Communicating: getting the point across

Inevitably, the two systems of thinking illustrated throughout this chapter influence the ways in which we communicate. Much of the time we are guided by the impressions from quick and easy System 1 thinking, so communication will be more effective if it grabs attention: using simple expressions or rhymes ('woes unite foes' instead of 'woes unite enemies'), or using bright clear colours for writing. It is also subject to the same biases. People respond to requests to pay off their credit card bills differently according to the anchor with which they are presented. Suggesting a low minimum payment leads to people paying less than if a high

---

**Box 11  The 9-dot problem**

Using no more than four straight lines, and without lifting the pen from the paper, connect all the dots in the diagram below.

•   •   •

•   •   •

•   •   •

See Box 13 for solutions.

minimum payment is suggested, and ends with lower actual payments overall. The higher the suggested minimum payment, or anchor, the more people pay, and the greater the chance that they will pay off their bill completely.

The processes that underlie thinking clearly influence our understanding and our behaviour. The *theory of linguistic relativity* suggested that language fosters habits of perception as well as thinking and that different views of reality were reflected in different languages: Eskimos supposedly had many different words for snow. However this claim has been described by Steven Pinker as The Great Eskimo Vocabulary Hoax, with no supporting evidence behind it. We can understand the distinctions made in languages other than our own, but linguistic information alone does not prove the point. The experiment in Box 12 demonstrates how a combination of clear thinking, accurate observations, and cultural awareness may help to provide an answer to such questions.

## Concluding points

Work on the cognitive skills involved in thinking, reasoning, and communicating is still expanding, focusing for instance on the acquisition and development of these abilities, problems arising with them, interactions between them, and associated activities in the brain. Perhaps the point to emphasize is that, in order to function well and adapt as we go, we need to achieve a balance between knowing when to snap into action and when to stop and think. If we operated entirely on the basis of logic, like a computer, we would be unable to adapt flexibly to the complexities and uncertainties of the everyday world. Hence there are still some respects in which our abilities appear superior to those of artificially intelligent machines, even though the machines may have larger memories and be able to test hypotheses faster than us. In particular, of course, we have feelings as well as thoughts, which may help us to understand why we do the things that we do.

## Box 12  Does language influence the acquisition of mental skills?

Children speaking Asian languages do consistently better at mathematics than English-speaking children and their number words reflect a base-10 system (e.g. 12 is represented as 'ten-two'). First year school children from three Asian and three Western countries were asked to stack blue blocks, representing 10 units, and white blocks representing 1 unit, into piles to show particular numbers. More Asian than Western children made two correct constructions for each number. The Asian children used two blocks representing 10 units more than the Western children, and the Western children used the single-unit blocks more than the Asian children.

*Conclusion:* language differences may influence mathematical skills.

The evidence is strengthened by the finding that bilingual Asian-American children also score more highly on mathematical tests than do those who speak only English.

Miura and colleagues (1994).


## Box 13  Solutions

Solution to bat and ball problem: 5 cents.

Solution to 9-dot problem, Box 11: This problem can only be solved by continuing some of the lines outside the boundary of the square defined by the dots, or by breaking the 'boundary' in some other way: e.g. cutting the dots into three rows and arranging them in one continuous line.

# Chapter 5
# Why do we do what we do? Motivation and emotion

Feelings do not just give colour to our experience, or provide the emotional weather through which we travel. They serve a purpose. They provide an impetus to action, and we often explain our actions in terms of those things that we felt at the time: I thumped the table because I was angry, avoided speaking because I felt nervous, or found myself a drink because I was thirsty. Motivations (hunger, thirst, sex) determine the goals towards which I strive, and emotions (happiness, frustration, despair) reflect the feelings I experience along the way. In previous chapters we have thought about how the brain receives, stores, and works with information collected from the external world so that we can perceive, pay attention, learn, remember, think, and so on. But of course the brain is an integral part of the body in which we experience the feelings that accompany motivation and emotion. Needless to say, we are not aware of much of the neural activity that is going on when moved by our feelings, nor of the ways in which they interact with the processes of perception and cognition. Nevertheless, these *affective* processes help to explain why we do what we do. All these activities taking place in the brain have evolved so that when they function well they help us to get what we want and to avoid what we do not want, so motivations and emotions influence the way we behave, whether that means taking action or deciding not to do so.

## Motivation: the pushes and prods

George Miller defined motivation as: 'all those pushes and prods—biological, social and psychological—that defeat our laziness and move us, either eagerly or reluctantly, to action'. The motives behind our actions are guided by several forces: hunger is a biological motive, acceptance a social one, and curiosity a psychological one. So motivation is complex. Hunger, for example, is determined by external as well as internal factors—by the smell of newly cooked bread as well as by the emptiness of the stomach. If I am hungry I look for food, and the hungrier I am the harder I look and the longer I look. Hunger determines the direction, intensity, and persistence of my behaviour—but it does not determine all aspects of my eating behaviour. I may also look for something to eat when I have an ache in my heart and not in my stomach, or just because I have a habit of doing so when I return home.

Understanding the intricacies of motivation is based on recognizing that its workings have evolved so as to help us to minimize physical pain and to maximize pleasure, something that the mechanics of reinforcement help us to do (see also Chapter 3). If I eat when I am unhappy as well as when I am hungry, this is because it makes me feel better. My personal experience of the reinforcement contingencies involved has associated reducing the pain of unhappiness, as well as that of hunger, with the satisfaction (or pleasure) that comes from eating. So signals that rewards might be available play a central part in explanations of behaviour, and in explanations of variations in behaviour.

The processes that determine responses to reward signals are fundamental, and they have a biological basis in the brain. Nerve cells in the midbrain that release the neurotransmitter dopamine signal 'reward' by becoming more active immediately after a reward, such as receiving satisfying food or drink. However, the brain works in a rather more complex way, using its ability to base predictions about the future on the sum of past experience. The calculations that it makes, according to this *affective prediction hypothesis*, are similar to those described for perceptual processes in Chapter 2, and they are illustrated in the study described next. Patterns of neural activity experienced in the past are coded and stored in such a way as to determine expectations about the future, and their responses are sensitive to whether or not those expectations are fulfilled.

Activity in dopamine-releasing cells was recorded during an experiment in which a signal (a flash of light) was associated with a squirt of fruit juice into a monkey's mouth. The cells responded immediately to the (rewarding) squirt of juice. After a while the same cells started to respond earlier, immediately after the light flash that signalled the arrival of juice. Activity in the cells then preceded and predicted the expected reward, rather than responding to it. When the light flash continued but the monkeys were given no juice, activity in these dopamine-releasing cells declined. The suggestion is that the information provided by changes in activity in these cells indicates when there is an error in the prediction about reward. If the reward arrives as expected, the prediction is accurate and the background pattern of activity in the cell does not change. If the juice arrives unexpectedly, or if it fails to arrive at all, the prediction is wrong and signals from the cell change accordingly. They respond more if the reward is delivered and less if it is not, thus providing information about what to expect in the future. The details of this experiment, illustrating the different patterns of cell activity, are shown in Figure 10.

Observations such as this suggest that all experiences, every event, object, and place encountered, are associated with a particular value, reflected in the activity of specific, dopamine-releasing brain cells. The value that something has for us determines whether or not we want it, are motivated to seek it out, and will

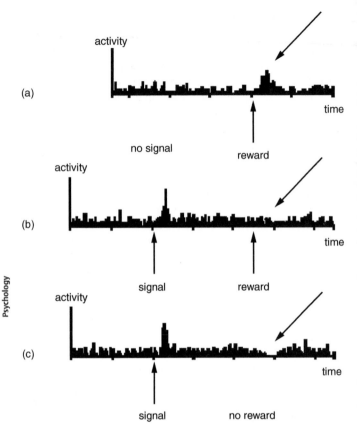

10. Reward signalling by dopamine neurons. Activity in dopamine neurons represents the error in our prediction of reward

(a) there was no signal so the monkey doesn't know when the reward will come. The unpredicted reward causes an increase in activity
(b) The monkey knew when the reward would come. The reward causes no change in activity. But the monkey doesn't know when the signal will come. The unpredicted signal of reward causes an increase in activity
(c) The monkey expects the reward to come, but it doesn't. The lack of the predicted reward causes a decrease in activity

take action to get it. Some of the things that we seek are inherently valuable to all animals: sleep, food, air, water, and sex, and taking action to get them is necessary for survival. Genetics and experience contribute a degree of variation in motivation, but these *primary reinforcers* usually retain the value they have acquired through years of evolution. Using the ability to make predictions, human beings, and other animals also, are able to make links between the things they value and others that are associated with them (the light flash in the experiment described above), so that the associated experiences (smells, events, objects, places, etc.) acquire a value of their own and become *secondary reinforcers*. Primary and secondary reinforcers, once their value is established, work in the same way. We have all experienced habituation to specific rewards, so, for example, we no longer respond if we have had too much of a good thing (satiation) and we respond strongly if deprived of it.

The suggestion here is that reward-processing regions of the brain act as a common neural interface to action across species. Of course this is only part of the story, and there is as yet no adequate theory of motivation that accounts for all that is now known about human motivation. When it comes to understanding why we do what we do, we need to encompass both types of reinforcement: reflecting the value to us of satisfying physiological needs (that help us survive), as well as the value to us of satisfying higher level needs in which cognitive factors are important, such as the desire to be liked and successful. Two contrasting theories illustrate the ways in which psychologists have thought about motivation: *homeostatic drive theory* and *goal theory*.

The basic idea in homeostatic drive theory is that it is important to maintain a reasonably constant internal environment. Any move away from this, or imbalance, prompts action to restore the balanced state. The action is 'driven' by the sense of imbalance, and continues until the balance is restored: the physiological effects of hunger send us to the kitchen, and eating what we find there reduces the disequilibrium, or discomfort, caused by the hunger. *Drive reduction theory* incorporates ideas about reinforcement into this basic homeostatic theory, suggesting that behaviours that successfully reduce a drive, like eating when you are hungry, will be experienced as pleasurable and thus be reinforced. The motivation to continue the behaviour decreases as the drive is satisfied. We should therefore slow down or stop eating when no longer hungry. What we actually do will depend on a combination of motivation (the hunger drive) and learning. Some foods, like chocolates, are easy to go on eating even when no longer hungry. The theory explains some aspects of complex behavioural patterns (for example, refusing to eat so as to get attention) quite well. Satisfying the need for attention may help, in this example, to re-establish a normal pattern of eating. However, the notion of drives does not apply to other aspects of behaviour such as tasting a new Mexican salsa or eating the parsnips so as not to cause offence. Social, cognitive, and aesthetic factors motivate much of our behaviour, and these cannot be explained by drive reduction theory without postulating a drive to match every contingency: a drive to listen to Schubert, and another for listening to Miles Davis, or to walk along the top of the hill.

In contrast, *goal theory* attempts to explain why we do what we do in terms of cognitive factors, suggesting that the key to someone's motivation is what they are consciously trying to do: their goal. This theory suggests that people will work harder, and use more resources, when the goal is harder to achieve, and the harder the goal, the higher the level of performance. An experiment testing this theory in the work place is described in Box 14.

Goal setting has been shown to improve performance in 90 per cent of the relevant studies, and it is especially likely to do so under the following conditions: people accept the goals set, they are informed about their progress, they are rewarded for achieving goals, they have the ability to reach them, and they are appropriately supported and encouraged by those in charge. These findings have been usefully applied in work settings, although we

> ### Box 14 Doing your best
>
> *Hypothesis*: People given the hardest goal should perform best.
>
> *Method*: Three sets of workers were given the task of cutting and transporting wood, working in small groups. The 'do your best' groups were given no goal; the 'assigned' groups were given a pre-assigned, hard goal; and 'participative' groups were required to set their own specific hard goal.
>
> *Result*: The 'do your best' group transported 46 cubic feet of wood an hour, compared with 53 cubic feet for the 'assigned' group and 56 cubic feet for the 'participative' group.
>
> Latham and Yukl (1975).

still need to know why some workers set higher goals than others, and how the motivating forces mobilized by setting a goal interact with others (physiological, social, and so on). Research findings in this field have many practical applications, for example in helping us to motivate people to learn and to work, and helping us to understand and combat difficulties in motivational systems, such as those that result in obesity and difficulties in dieting.

## Emotion

While motivations determine our goals, emotions reflect the feelings we experience when we have succeeded, or failed, in meeting our goals. All manner of feelings may be experienced along the way: in anticipation, at the time, or afterwards, and these feelings are a product of the neural interface to action which has interested numerous psychologists (at least) since the 19th century. This is a field full of complexities, partly because the different components of emotion do not consistently correlate with each other. The five components are *physiological* (heart rate and blood pressure changes), *expressive* (smiling, frowning, slumping in a chair), *behavioural* (making a fist, running away), *cognitive* (perceiving a threat, remembering a loss, thinking about a pleasure), and *experiential* (the complex of feelings experienced). I can smile when I am sad and feel fearful before I have consciously perceived a threat, and this lack of correlation means that emotion cannot be properly studied or understood by measuring any one of its components. A further complicating factor is that two independent processes contribute to determining individual subjective experience: the level of arousal determines the intensity of a feeling, while contextual and cognitive factors determine its valence (positive or negative value) and precise nature.

Cross-cultural and cross-species research initiated by Charles Darwin shows that facial expressions associated with fear, anger, sadness, surprise, disgust, and happiness are sufficiently similar to be recognizable in people from different ethnic groups and in some animals (Figure 11). However a much greater variety of emotions can be identified at the experiential than at the

**11. A primary emotion recognizable in one of the gargoyles on an Oxford college**

physiological or expressive levels: there are as many types of smile and frown as there are people to express them and situations to provoke them. Furthermore, complex emotions like guilt and shame, which are strongly determined by cognitive factors such as what we think about ourselves, what we think others think, and by internalized social rules, are difficult to recognize accurately. Besides, we usually experience mixtures of emotions rather than pure states. Although there are common aspects of these feelings, so that you and I can both feel sad, recognize it in each other, and talk about it, our experiences of sadness will differ. The meaning that it has for me, and the way in which I express it, is determined by how it fits into my world right now, by my past experience, memories, thoughts, and reactions, and by how others have previously reacted to my sadness—by the pattern of firing in my brain cells that reflects the expectations and predictions derived from my personal experience. If others have told me to go away and stop bothering them I may hide it or find it hard to talk about. An investigation of interactions between emotion, bodily sensations, and cognition found that if the emotion triggered by a particular event is both experienced and expressed (behaviourally or verbally), then the event is remembered better than if the emotion is experienced but not expressed. It sounds as if the act of expressing an emotion provides a stronger (cognitive) memory trace—or conversely, that keeping a stiff upper lip interferes with memory for emotional events.

There are many ways of understanding the interactions between thoughts and feelings. According to the James-Lange theory of emotion, which is well over 100 years old, changes in bodily responses are necessary for emotional experience, so sadness arises from crying and fear from running away, rather than the other way round. This can sound counter-intuitive, as people tend to believe that they feel sad because of what has happened to them, or because of what they are thinking about or remembering. In this century it has become possible to identify and to measure minute bodily (neural) changes, and to demonstrate how bodily arousal, and the feelings associated with both motivation and emotion, interact with cognition, subjective experience, and behaviour. Fine-grained neuro-psychological studies have revealed how the brain operates in sufficient detail to map the 'functional architecture' that links cognition and emotion. Much neural activity is generated automatically, and remains out of awareness. Laboratory studies have shown that it takes between 200 and 350 milliseconds for us to become consciously aware of incoming sensory information. Research on facial recognition shows that in under 200 milliseconds we can distinguish a face from a non-face, and categorize it as happy, sad, or neutral. So, information about affect is one of the basic ingredients being fed into all mental activity, and it links up with the processes of perception, attention, learning, and cognition described in the previous chapters. We know that the brain captures statistical regularities, learns how to discriminate the familiar from the new, makes predictions, and learns from errors. We now know that activity in the parts of the brain associated with emotion and with motivation is organized on the same general principles.

Successful theories should provide an explanation of how we know that the situation we are in is dangerous, exciting, or safe as well as a description of what is happening in the brain. A different approach to this problem is illustrated by *cognitive labelling theory* (or *two factor theory*). According to this theory, emotional experience is determined by a combination of physiological arousal and the *labelling*, or interpretation, of the sensations experienced during that arousal. In order to test this theory ingenious experiments were devised that involved varying some components of emotion while holding others constant, as described in Box 15. The findings from these experiments show that what we experience is greatly influenced by cognitive factors: by what we know about a situation, how we interpret what happens to us internally and externally, and of course what we have learned and remembered about such situations in the past.

### Box 15  Do I know what I feel?

*Aim*: To find out what will happen when people have similar physiological symptoms of arousal but experience emotionally different situations.

*Method*: Some research participants, supposedly taking part in a test of the effects of a new vitamin on visual skills, were injected with adrenaline (which is physiologically arousing) and others were injected with a saline solution. Only some of those injected with adrenaline were correctly informed of its effects. While waiting for the drug to take effect the participants were put in a situation designed to produce either euphoria or anger (using a stooge).

*Results*: After the waiting period, the emotion the participants reported reflected the mood expressed by the stooge, and was clearly influenced by social and cognitive factors. Those who had received the adrenaline injection but had not been correctly informed of its effects were most emotional. They were most likely later to report feeling relatively happy or irritable, according to how the stooge had behaved. Those who had been correctly informed responded less strongly to the behaviour of the stooge and appeared to attribute their experience at least partly to the injection.

*Conclusion*: Our awareness of the situation we are in influences the emotion that we actually feel, but our physiological state *determines how strongly we feel it.*

Schachter and Singer (1962).

Despite flaws in these early experiments, cognitive labelling theory had a major impact, and subsequent research into cognitive aspects of emotion has contributed much to the understanding of emotional distress and to the development of psychological treatments. Cognitive-behavioural therapies, particularly for depression and anxiety, are based on the idea that thoughts, feelings, and behaviour are so intimately related that changing one will change the others. As it is difficult to change feelings directly, cognitive-behavioural therapies attempt to change them indirectly by working in therapy to change thinking, finding new ways of seeing things or developing new perspectives, and testing these out in practice. For example, the loss of a relationship may be interpreted as meaning that I will never find another partner (a thought which makes me sad, and which makes it hard for me to get out and meet more people), but it could also be interpreted as meaning that, although I am understandably upset, I still have the characteristics that my lost partner found attractive and can still make new friends. In other words, understanding more about the cognitive aspects of emotion has helped us to understand more of the intricacies of the relationships between thoughts, feelings, and behaviour in general. In turn, this has guided the development of cognitive-behavioural therapies which are demonstrably effective in helping people who are experiencing a wide range of emotional difficulties.

There is evidence that the part of the brain called the *limbic system* functions as an emotional centre, and that the layers of convoluted grey matter (*cortex* and *neocortex*) developed later in evolutionary terms, thereby adding the ability to think about feelings, amongst other things. Information travels speedily and directly into and out of the limbic system, only reaching centres of cognition later, thus making us susceptible to 'emotional hijacking': the burst of anger or paroxysm of fear that overtakes us despite our having decided to remain calm and in control of our sensibilities. In extreme fear we may react 'primitively' by running away, or more thoughtfully by helping others first. A primitive reaction to hunger might involve eating anything available and a more reasoned one involves 'holding back' or not 'giving in'. So strategic behaviours are needed to combat the pressure from more primitive systems, and these give rise to all manner of complex emotions ranging from self-satisfaction to unsatisfied longing.

The evolutionarily primitive aspect of emotion helps to explain its power to disrupt thinking. When we are emotionally upset and complain that we can no longer think straight we are in fact quite correct. The frontal lobes play an important part in working memory, and they cannot function well when activation in the limbic system is dominant and demands full attention. This observation focused the attention of psychologists on finding out how control over emotions is acquired, and it has many practical applications, such as helping to change attitudes towards disruptive children who are slow to learn. Those who are distressed and disturbed will find it difficult to learn because of their high degree of emotional arousal, and their potential for school learning can be enhanced by alleviating their distress as much as or more than by increased teaching.

For many years experimental psychologists paid little systematic attention to feelings, assuming that useful explanations of human behaviour were more likely to be found elsewhere. Indeed, we do sometimes speak as though feelings get in the way, or complain that they interfere with otherwise rational behaviour, and some psychologists seem to have assumed that feelings were more properly the province of clinicians, whose understanding of feelings is informed by personal qualities such as sensitivity and the ability to empathize as well as by their knowledge of the more scientific aspects of psychology. This view, however, gives insufficient weight to the evolutionary functions of motivation and emotion.

Fear organizes us for flight; anger for attack. Of course, feelings such as anger can get us into as well as out of trouble, but without them we might put ourselves at risk; and we also depend on them for defining goals and organizing ourselves to work towards them. It has been argued that there is such a thing as emotional intelligence—a quality that varies between people and that can be more or less successfully employed to help us achieve our aims. Definitions of emotional intelligence are varied, placing more or less emphasis on self-awareness and on perceptiveness about others, and it is unclear whether it represents a predetermined personality trait or an ability that can be acquired. The hypothesis that a higher level of emotional intelligence will contribute to better social adjustment and to positive mental health does not (yet) have unambiguous support.

In summary, the study of motivation and emotion has contributed to clinical fields as widely diverse as those of psychoanalysis and humanistic or cognitive-behavioural therapies, and to the development of programmes for those who need help with the regulation of eating, drinking, and sexual behaviours, and with addictive behaviours such as smoking and gambling. It has contributed because, in order to study feelings and to answer questions about why we do what we do, it has proved necessary to think in terms of many interacting systems: physical, cognitive, affective, behavioural, and socio-cultural. The complexity of doing this means that there is still much to learn.

Our increased understanding of the interactions between emotional arousal and the capacity to attend, learn, and remember has had some practical uses. For example, in the UK the Courts do not currently accept evidence collected using lie detectors, which only measure one component of emotion and therefore cannot be reliable. The complexity of the field may explain why there is still debate about such important issues as the effects of watching scenes of violence on television and the question of whether it is better to bottle up anger or to express it.

# Chapter 6

# Is there a set pattern? Developmental psychology

The most obvious way that people develop is physical: transforming from tiny, helpless babies into more or less capable adults. Of course we go on changing throughout our lives, but here we focus predominantly on early development—on changes that lead to maturation. Psychological studies in this area have revealed typical patterns of development, and their findings are used to predict the effects of early experience on later behaviour; to advise parents about what to expect at different ages; to ascertain when development is not progressing as it should, and to plan appropriate opportunities to maximize developmental potential (e.g. ameliorating the effects of social disadvantage on education).

Developmental psychology is concerned with understanding both what changes occur with age, and how those changes take place—the *process* of development. Two questions are particularly important in looking at the process of development. First, does development take place in stages or is the process more continuous, or more variable, than that? And, second, is development biologically determined by 'nature' (the genetically programmed process of physical maturation) or influenced by environmental circumstances (by 'nurture')? The concept of stages suggests that everyone passes through the same stages in the same order, reaching the later ones only by going through earlier ones.

It clearly is necessary to acquire basic before complex skills, and rough stages of development are reflected in the terms 'baby', 'child', and 'adult'. But are there also finer stages? If so, how flexible are they? Observation suggests that development is not as fixed as the idea of stages suggests: most children crawl before they can walk, but some do not.

Exceptions to expected patterns of development prompted developmental psychologists to propose that there are *critical* (or at least *sensitive*) *periods* in human development—that is, time periods during which events must occur, or not occur, for development to proceed normally. For example, if a human foetus does not receive the correct hormones before the 7th week of gestation, a genetic male may fail to develop male sexual organs until puberty triggers another bout of hormonal activity. By this time they may have already developed a female identity and find it difficult to adjust to a male one. Similarly it is easier to learn a second language fluently, without an accent, as a child than it is as an adult; and case studies of 'feral children', raised without exposure to language, suggest that children who have not started to learn a language by about the age of 7 may struggle to learn it at all.

The relative importance of genetic and environmental factors—the nature/nurture question—is especially relevant to developmental psychology. Similarities in the characteristics of genetically identical twins reared apart suggest strong genetic influences on development. However, it is clear that the environment also influences development—the potential to learn a spoken language may be inborn (nature component), but the specific language learnt is determined by the person's environment (nurture component). Indeed the environment, including social and cultural norms, may influence not only whether it is English or Chinese that is learnt and the accent with which it is spoken, but also the rate of language learning (children who are spoken to frequently acquire language sooner than those who are not). Just to complicate things further, there are interactions between genes and the environment—babies born with happy dispositions may elicit more positive responses from caregivers, thereby influencing their environment, which in turn exerts further influence on their temperamental development—happy smiley children elicit more positive responses from caregivers and thus become more happy and smiley.

## What is inborn?

As mentioned in Chapter 3, babies are born predisposed to learn. They are born with useful reflexes such as sucking and grasping, and by 1 month babies can discriminate sounds in order to gain a sweet taste. In all species, the young appear to be primed to learn skills that are useful—and human babies may be 'set up' with abilities that encourage caregiving from adults. For example, newborn babies' exceptional ability to discriminate speech sounds allows them to recognize and show a preference for their mother's voice by the time they are 3 days old. It is even possible that some learning takes place in the womb—newborn babies respond differently to their mother's language than to other languages. However, an 'innate' potential (or ability) may guide and facilitate subsequent learning. The experiment in Box 16 suggests that babies are born able to organize and interpret the flood of sensory stimuli they experience, as if they were already using some elementary perceptual principles (such as those described in Chapter 2).

Similarly, recent research suggests that babies may not be as innocent as they appear. It was thought that children did not understand that other people could hold a different viewpoint ('theory of mind'), and thus that children did not develop the ability to deceive until the age of 3 or 4 years old. However, more recent studies show that children as young as 15 months can have some understanding of false beliefs, and that even 6-month-old babies may use this strategically by engaging in fake crying to gain attention. And their deceit becomes more sophisticated with

## Box 16 What do babies know about numbers?

Some 6–8-month-old babies were shown a series of pairs of slides, one showing three and the other showing two objects. At the same time as the babies were seeing a pair of slides, a speaker played either two or three drumbeats. The babies tended to look longer at the slide that matched the number of drumbeats. So when there were two drumbeats the babies spent more time looking at the slide with two objects. These results suggested that babies can abstract numerical information sufficiently well to recognize similarity or to 'match' like with like.

Similar experiments with 9-month-olds have suggested that babies show more surprise when sums don't add up—for example, when two lots of five objects go behind a box but only one lot is still there when the box is lifted. It is not suggested that they have specific knowledge about numbers, or about adding and subtracting, but rather that they have some innate ability that helps them to learn about these.

Starkey, Spelke, and Gelman (1990) and McCrink and Wynn (2004).

age—by 8 months they may attempt to conceal forbidden activities or to distract a parent from seeing them. There is also evidence that babies may have some understanding of social dominance and hierarchy by as young as 10 months—they look for longer when a big person concedes to a smaller person than vice versa; and toddlers more often attempt to take a toy from a child smaller than themselves than from a bigger child.

## Brain development

More developmental changes occur in the first few years of life than in any other time period—by the age of 2 you will be approximately half your adult height and your brain will be 80 per cent of its adult size. You will also be able to walk and feed yourself, and use language to communicate basic needs. However, the brain continues to develop both in structure and function for far longer. Although it reaches its maximum weight by the age of 19–21 it continues to develop for several more years. For example, one of the last regions to become fully formed, around the age of 25, is the region that inhibits risky behaviour. Brain imaging studies suggest that motivation and reward circuitry in adolescent brains make them more prone to risk-taking behaviours such as substance abuse and unsafe sex, and more vulnerable to addictions and poor impulse control. As well as changes in structure, the neural pathways in the brain change with age—a 3-year-old's brain has about twice as many neural connections as an adult brain, and during adolescence a process of 'pruning' starts, with those connections that are unnecessary or inefficient being lost. During adolescence, the amount of myelin (a fatty, insulating material that coats the axons of nerve cells) also increases, improving the nerve cells' ability to conduct electrical signals and to function efficiently. This too continues into adulthood and occurs later in 'higher' regions of the brain, such as the prefrontal cortex.

## Personality and social development

Two-month-old babies of different cultures, and even blind babies, smile at their caregivers—an action that is likely to strengthen the bond between them, although initially it could be reflexive rather than communicative. The universality of smiling suggests that maturation may be important in determining its onset. Then, by 3 or 4 months, babies recognize and prefer familiar people although they remain friendly towards strangers until about 8 to 12 months old, when a fear of strangers develops. Both distress on separation and fear of strangers decrease by the age of 2 or 3, when children are more able to take care of some of their own needs. These changes make evolutionary sense: the fear of strangers increases with mobility and then decreases with increasing capability.

It has been suggested that the child's bond with its *primary caregiver* (the person who does the majority of the caring for the child) is crucial in determining later psychological development: 'mother love in infancy and childhood is as important for mental health as are vitamins and proteins for physical health' (Bowlby, 1951). This bond is often referred to as an *attachment*—that is, a relatively enduring emotional tie to a specific person (the *attachment figure*). An interesting hypothesis suggests that if this primary attachment relationship is not adequate, then serious psychiatric disorder may follow in adulthood. Secure attachments may enable children to feel secure in exploring new settings, gradually increasing their independence and *detachment* from the attachment figure.

Attachment can be measured by how much the child seeks to be near the attachment figure, and is generally oriented towards them, becoming upset when they leave and happy when they return. Developmental psychologists have classified the quality of 12–18-month-old children's attachments by observing their behaviour in a structured setting, called the *strange situation*, in which a child and its caregiver (usually the mother) are in a room full of toys. After some time, they are joined by someone who is a stranger to the child; then the caregiver leaves and returns a short while later. The child's behaviour is observed at all stages through a one-way mirror. The child's responses to the caregiver leaving and returning, and to the presence of the stranger are used to classify the child's attachment style, the main categories being secure, avoidant, or resistant/ambivalent. Securely attached children are able to use their caregiver's presence as a safe base for exploration and protest at their departure. They can be somewhat comforted by the stranger but are clearly more attached to the caregiver and immediately seek and gain comfort from them on their return. In contrast, children showing a more avoidant attachment pattern treat the stranger and the caregiver similarly—they are little affected by the caregiver leaving and are as easily comforted by the stranger as the caregiver. An ambivalent/resistant attachment pattern is characterized by the child having difficulty in using the caregiver as a safe base for exploration, and showing distress on separation but ambivalence or anger on the caregiver's return. These children also resist the stranger's attempts to comfort them and appear preoccupied with the caregiver's availability. Theories about attachment have provided a rich source of hypotheses for subsequent research, for example on attachment behaviours, on the behaviour of caregivers—whether male or female—and on possible links between attachment history and responses to events and experiences later in life.

Although initially it was thought that attachment behaviour was a form of 'cupboard love'—that children became attached to their caregivers primarily because they were the main source of food, experiments with monkeys such as the one in Box 17 suggest that this is not the case.

In humans, it seems that the most important factors influencing attachment are the child's temperament (its 'nature') and the attachment figure's *responsiveness*: understanding of and sensitivity

### Box 17  Is attachment just 'cupboard love'?

Infant monkeys were separated from their mothers shortly after birth and were given two substitute 'mothers'. Both substitute mothers were made from wire mesh with wooden heads. One was covered with foam padding and terrycloth, which made it more cuddly. The other was bare wire but dispensed milk from a bottle attached to its chest. The monkeys showed much more attachment to the cuddly mother in spite of the fact that it was the 'wire' mother that gave them milk. (See Figure 12.)

Harlow (1958).

**12. Attachment in monkeys**

to the child's needs. The attachment figures of insecurely attached babies tend to respond more on the basis of their own needs than to the baby's signals. For example, they play with the baby when it is convenient for them rather than when the baby shows signs of wanting to play. This may explain why a child's strongest attachment is not necessarily to the person who does most of the physical caretaking—the quality of care may be more important than the quantity in determining the particular style of attachments.

# Effects of early experience

An important enterprise for developmental psychology has been to try to determine whether early experiences such as deprivation or attachment history affect later development, and if the effects can be ameliorated. The experiments in Box 18 attempt to investigate this issue.

## Box 18 Investigating the effects of early deprivation and abuse

In the 1960s, psychologist Harry Harlow and colleagues carried out a series of studies investigating the effects of early deprivation and abuse on monkeys. They found that depriving monkeys of social interaction from birth, by raising them where they can see but not touch other monkeys, led to highly maladaptive behaviour. Monkeys raised in such conditions were socially withdrawn and aggressive to their peers, they had difficulty mating, and often subsequently became abusive to their own offspring. However, if the monkeys were reintegrated by 3 months, or if they were given even one playmate, they could develop normally. Other experiments involved raising monkeys with 'abusive mothers'—which were cloth monkeys that blasted the infants with cold air. These studies found that the abused baby monkeys showed stronger attachments to their 'mothers' than non-abused monkeys.

Although it would be unethical to carry out such experiments with human babies, it is possible to study individual case studies of extreme deprivation or abuse, and children who spend significant amounts of time in institutions. Such studies show that the effects of deprivation in childhood are not clear cut—there is much evidence that children raised in extremely poor environments, such as institutions with low staff ratios and high turnover, or with animals, are severely disadvantaged in terms of their physical, cognitive, and social development.

Yet there are also studies, such as those on children from Romanian orphanages adopted by English families before the age of 2, which show remarkable 'catch up' of abilities by the age of 4. The catch up effect was strongest for the children who were adopted earlier (by the age of 6 months). However, early deprivation also appeared to have a long-term impact as the children tended to form disinhibited attachments, showing indiscriminate friendliness to any adult.

Cases of extreme neglect have also been used to help understand the reversibility of early deprivation. 'Genie' spent most of her first 13 years alone, tightly bound, and being beaten for making any sound. When she was discovered, Genie could neither chew nor walk upright, was incontinent, and understood little language. She was given intensive rehabilitation and eventually placed in a foster home where she made amazing progress in developing both physical and social skills. However, although she learnt to understand and use basic language, her grammar and pronunciation remained abnormal, and her progress deteriorated when she later returned to institutional care. In contrast, Koluchova describes the case of 7-year-old twin boys who were discovered in similarly extreme conditions but who did seem to make a remarkable recovery, and were able to live normal adult lives after being placed in an exceptionally caring foster family. The differences in outcome may be due to a combination of risk and rescue factors such as inherent resilience, the availability of one caring person, the age at 'rescue', and the quality of rehabilitative care. Many studies show that the harmful effects of early experiences can be ameliorated, at least somewhat, particularly if the child is still young when the conditions are improved. However, it is difficult to draw conclusions from such studies as of course there are no directly comparable control groups (we cannot randomly allocate half the children to be deprived or abused!) and it is not usually known whether those who ended up in deprived environments had any disabilities prior to these experiences.

Research also shows that later experiences have an impact on the relationship between early experiences and later outcomes. Children raised in care ended up with much better functioning if they had positive school experiences and marriages. Such research has led to changes in the recommended ways that children are cared for in institutions (e.g. emphasizing opportunities for social interaction as well as providing physical care), and in greater use of family foster care for children who cannot be cared for in their families of origin. Similarly, findings showing multiple attachments, and that the primary attachment does not have to be to the mother, have helped to resolve concerns about children raised in non-stereotypical families (e.g. by same sex parents).

## Development over the lifespan

Although this chapter has focused on early development, people continue to develop physically and psychologically throughout their lives. Whilst changes such as puberty are at least partly due to physical maturation, others reflect a substantial degree of environmental influence, such as adopting a more sedentary lifestyle with increasing age and retirement. Several developmental psychologists have proposed theories outlining the developmental stages across the lifespan and Table 1 outlines one of these. Erikson's theory suggests that there are definite stages, each involving a specific dilemma or *psychosocial crisis*, that everyone progresses through during a lifetime. However, subsequent research has suggested that the stages might not be as fixed as was initially thought, with, for example, some adolescents having a strong sense of identity.

In later life, the focus for developmental psychology has been on cognitive functioning. Initially, studies comparing intelligence test scores in groups of older and younger people showed that younger people had higher IQs, suggesting that intelligence declined with age. However, these studies failed to take account of the *cohort effect*—social determinants of performance on IQ

#### Table 1 Erikson's (1968) Stages of development

| Stage | Main task or challenge associated with the stage |
|---|---|
| Early infancy (1st year of life) | Trust vs. mistrust. Trusting and risking disappointment vs. being mistrustful and not relating fully to others. This balance is affected by both the child's disposition and the quality of caregiving. |
| Later infancy (1–3 years) | Autonomy vs. shame. Developing a sense of autonomy and personal responsibility vs. the sense of shame arising from doubt about one's abilities. |
| Early childhood (3–6 years) | Initiative vs. guilt. Increased personal responsibility for and initiative in making one's own choices vs. guilt about those choices. |
| Middle childhood (6–11 years) | Industry vs. inferiority. Learning to exert effort to overcome challenges and developing competence, with reference to others and to perceived norms (in the classroom or family) vs. fearing challenge and feeling inadequate or a failure. |
| Adolescence (12–18 years) | Identity vs. role confusion. Establishing a consistent sense of identity through exploration of different roles vs. confusion from overwhelming opportunities and failure to develop an integrated self-image. |
| Young adulthood (18–35) | Intimacy vs. isolation. Exploring romantic and other attachments to experience love and commitment vs. fearing relationships and risking isolation and loneliness. |

| Mature adulthood (35–64) | Generativity vs. stagnation. Developing productivity in contributing to family and society vs. stagnation and feelings of uselessness. |
| --- | --- |
| Late adulthood (65 onwards) | Ego integrity vs. despair. Being able to look back at one's life with a sense of integrity and accomplishment vs. looking back with a sense of despair. |

tests and the fact that intelligence scores of the whole population had increased with better education and nutrition. When intelligence was measured repeatedly in the same people there was no evidence that it declined with age; rather, it increased slightly for those who continued to use their minds. Similarly, the supposed deterioration of memory with age does not stand up well to scientific investigation but suggests that the system responds to the demands you make of it. Comparisons of memory for everyday events show that older people perform slightly better than younger ones, possibly because they are more concerned about their memories and are more attentive and motivated during testing. The belief that memory declines with increasing age was described as a myth in 2012, as it appears to be partly due to a self-fulfilling prophecy. If people expect to become more forgetful they try less hard and notice forgetting more than remembering—younger people are altogether less bothered by signs of forgetfulness. It appears that as long as people continue to keep physically, mentally, and socially active, they need not expect a noticeable decline in their mental abilities until very late in life (in the absence of conditions such as dementia). Indeed, the knowledge they have accumulated may help them to do better than younger people in some respects, although they are still likely to have trouble remembering names and appointments.

Many biological, social, and environmental factors influence developmental processes. Although there is a rough pattern for development, and self-righting tendencies stimulate constant adaptation, there are also many potential pitfalls. The process is clearly a complex one, so differences between age groups could result from changes over the generations rather than from ageing itself, and in adulthood the differences within age groups are usually far greater than those between them. Nevertheless developmental psychologists can make predictions about which factors will affect development adversely and which will not—in fields as diverse as moral development, language acquisition, and the development of thinking and gender identity. The challenges for developmental psychologists are to find ways of ameliorating the effects of negative early experiences, finding remedies for when development is not proceeding normally, and to explore ways of enhancing adjustment throughout the lifespan.

# Chapter 7

# Can we categorize people? Individual differences

While the previous chapter looked at typical developmental processes and patterns, emphasizing the similarities between people, this chapter is concerned with differences between people. Most of us prefer to think of ourselves as unique, but is it possible to categorize the differences between us, and to identify the determinants of such differences? On the practical side, psychologists have developed ways of measuring people so as to find out more about the similarities and differences between them. These psychological assessments often take the form of paper and pencil measures, such as aptitude or achievement tests, to measure abilities or accomplishments, or to assess suitability for particular educational or occupational positions.

## Psychological measurement

Psychological tests or *psychometric instruments* need to be both *reliable* and *valid*—that is, they should consistently measure the variable that they claim to measure. For example, a test of reading ability would not be considered a good test if it gave the same person very different scores when tested a few days apart (low reliability) or if a person who could not read well scored highly on it (low validity). To be useful, psychological tests must also be *standardized*, which means that there must be an established set of 'norms' against which to compare individual scores.

Standardizing tests involves giving the test to a large group of the type of people it is intended for, and using statistics to calculate *norms*—to work out what is an average score; and what proportion of the population score different amounts above or below this average. These norms can then be used to interpret an individual's test score. For instance, IQ (intelligence quotient) tests are scored so that the population's average score is 100, and 95 per cent of the population score between 70 and 130, so someone scoring 132 can be judged to be well above average (in the top 2.5 per cent). Psychologists have also found that the way in which a test is administered and the conditions of testing can influence the results. If the lighting is poor, or the person does not hear or understand the instructions, then their score may be artificially low. Thus, the conditions under which the test is administered must also be standardized—as far as possible the test must be given to each person in exactly the same way, under similar conditions, if the results are to be valid.

Psychometric tests are used to assess a wide variety of abilities and attributes, and this chapter focuses on the two facets of individual differences that have been most intensively studied and measured: intelligence and personality. As in other areas of psychology, there has been much debate about whether individual differences in intelligence and personality are the results of inherited or environmental influences (nature or nurture).

## Intelligence

Despite being one of the most important concepts in psychology, intelligence is one of the most elusive to define. Intelligence can simply be viewed as the ability to respond adaptively to one's environment, but this ability may involve many aspects—such as being able to think logically, rationally, and abstractly, as well as the ability to be creative and to learn, and to apply this learning in new situations. Psychologists have questioned whether intelligence is a common thread underlying all mental processes (a general factor) or whether it reflects several different more or less closely related factors. There are correlations between different types of intelligence, but the abilities of *idiot savants*—people with low IQs but with one extraordinary ability, such as being able to name the day of the week of any date in the last ten years—suggest that people can have vastly different abilities in different areas. Furthermore, a question of great practical interest has been whether intelligence is predetermined (inborn), or whether it can be learnt or enhanced.

## Intelligence tests

One of the simplest definitions of intelligence is to define it as 'what IQ tests measure'—a circular definition that raises issues concerning the relationship between IQ tests and definitions of intelligence. The way in which intelligence is defined influences the tests that are designed to measure it. For example, a *two-factor model* supposes that intelligence is made up of a general factor and specific factors, whereas other models suggest that there are a number of independent specific factors such as numerical reasoning, memory, musical ability, word fluency, visuo-spatial ability, perceptual speed, insight into oneself, and understanding of others—but no single general factor. Another approach has been to examine the processes involved in intelligence, such as the speed of processing, how information is represented internally, or the strategies used to solve problems.

Lack of agreement over the definition of intelligence makes it difficult to construct tools to measure it: any intelligence test is based on a particular definition or conceptualization of intelligence and thus reflects the biases of that conceptualization. For example, timed tests place more emphasis on the speed of processing, whereas other tests may be designed to measure separate 'specific factors' or a general ability. Box 19 gives some examples of the items used in intelligence tests.

## Box 19 What intelligence tests ask

Most intelligence tests contain several subscales, consisting of different types of questions. Some may simply ask for information with questions such as 'how many months are there in a year?' Other subscales may assess the person's memory by asking them to repeat increasingly long strings of numbers forwards or backwards, or assess their arithmetic by asking questions like 'raffle tickets cost 76 pence each, if I bought six tickets how much change would I get from £10?'. Vocabulary or comprehension may be assessed by asking for definitions of common words, or by asking what the similarity is between word pairs such as 'orange-banana' or 'reward-punishment' (you would need to say that they were both a means of influencing the behaviour of others to get the maximum points). Other subscales may involve arranging pictures in the best order so they tell a story, or may be more practical such as arranging blocks to copy a design or doing jigsaw-like puzzles.

Intelligence tests usually give a score expressed as an *intelligence quotient* or IQ. As mental ability increases during the first 18 years of life, the 'raw' test scores must be adjusted in the light of the person's chronological age. This is done with reference to norms for the person's age group. For children, scores are sometimes expressed as a *mental age*. Thus a particularly bright 7-year-old child, who performs as well as the average 10-year-old, could be said to have a chronological age of 7 but a mental age of 10.

Intelligence tests have been criticized on many grounds. A fundamental difficulty is that they do not measure intelligence itself, but attempt to measure the qualities that are thought to reflect it. They have been validated primarily in terms of educational achievement, which may be less of a product of intelligence and more a product of other factors such as social class, opportunity, and motivation. Furthermore, IQ test scores have been shown to be affected by temporary situational factors such as motivation and emotional state, and can be increased by practice, which casts doubt on how truly they measure intelligence.

A particularly controversial finding is that black Americans scored significantly lower than white Americans on standard intelligence tests—originally the gap was 15 points but this had narrowed to half that by the late 1980s. Indeed, most ethnic groups score lower than white middle-class groups on IQ tests. This finding has been interpreted by some as 'evidence' of the intellectual superiority of some races over others, but other observations, such as the finding that German babies fathered by black and white American soldiers have similar IQs, suggest that the difference in IQ scores is unlikely to be due to genetic inferiority/superiority. Similar differences in IQ scores are also found in relation to a child's parental income. It is much more likely that such differences between races and social classes reflect a deficit in standard IQ tests—they are biased in favour of the dominant (often white middle-class) culture. Indeed the whole concept of a test is culture-bound (see Figure 13) and likely to advantage cultures with school-based systems of education where tests are commonplace. There have been attempts to construct 'culture-fair' tests, which do not ask for culturally biased information and often don't use language at all (see Figure 14 for an example). However, it has proved almost impossible to be fair to more than one culture at a time as the concepts being tested are rarely culture free, even in non-verbal tests. For example some cultures would group an orange with a knife and a fish with a hook, whereas others would group 'tools' and 'food'.

One suggestion that reconciles some of the disagreement about what intelligence is, and whether it is inborn, is that there are two basic types of intelligence: one that reflects a genetic potential or an inborn basic ability, and another that is acquired or learnt as

13. 'You can't build a hut, you don't know how to find edible roots, and you know nothing about predicting the weather. In other words, you do *terribly* on our IQ test.'

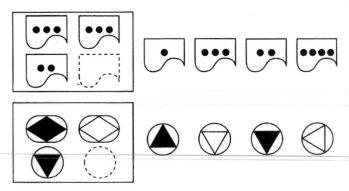

14. Culture-fair intelligence test questions. The participant is asked to choose which of the four items on the right best fits the pattern on the left

experience interacts with potential. In 1963, Cattell suggested that 'fluid' intelligence is the inborn ability to solve abstract problems, whereas 'crystallized' intelligence involves practical problem-solving and knowledge, which comes from experience.

## Is intelligence influenced by the environment?

Many studies show that those with the closest genetic relationship are also most similar in IQ scores, suggesting a strong genetic component to IQ. However, as genetic similarity between people increases so does similarity in their environments. One way of overcoming this is to study identical twins (who are genetically identical) who have been reared apart, comparing them with identical twins reared together. Those reared together have closer IQ scores, suggesting a role for the environment, and this is corroborated by studies of adopted children showing that their IQs are closer to those of their adoptive than biological parents. There is clearly a strong genetic influence as well, as the IQs of identical twins reared apart are still more similar than those of non-identical same-sex twins reared together. But, hardly surprisingly, it is not easy to separate the two types of influence. For instance, separated twins shared the same environment *in utero*, and the environment of an adopted child may intentionally be matched with that of its mother. The mother's IQ may contribute to the child's IQ in two ways: directly, through genetics, and indirectly, as her behaviour is one of the main determinants of the child's environment.

## Can intelligence be increased?

A question that is of greater practical use is whether intelligence can be enhanced by environmental influences. Even minimal interventions such as giving high quality nutritional supplements to children in developing countries can enhance IQ scores possibly through their effect on general health and, thus, on factors such as energy, concentration, and attention. There is also evidence showing that the amount of parental attention a child receives affects its IQ—this may explain why first-born children have slightly higher IQs than their siblings, because the first child usually gets more attention. Many studies have investigated whether various 'brain training' programmes can enhance IQ, and although they do enhance performance on certain tasks, there is little evidence that this effect generalizes to other tasks or persists once the training is discontinued, so it seems more of a 'practice effect' than any real enhancement of intelligence.

More practically focused studies have attempted to use educational programmes to help disadvantaged children; an example is provided in Box 20.

What can be concluded from these studies on intelligence and IQ? It seems likely that intelligence, which is still hard to define and to measure, is too complex a construct to be reflected in a single number such as an IQ score. On the practical side, studies of intelligence have shown that both genetic and environmental influences are important, and that it is possible to manipulate environmental circumstances to produce enduring benefits, both in terms of IQ and achievement.

## Personality

As a concept, personality is possibly even more central in psychology, and even more difficult to define, than intelligence. Loosely speaking, personality reflects a characteristic set of behaviours, attitudes, interests, motives, and feelings about the world. It includes the way in which people relate to others and is thought to be relatively stable throughout life. One reason for identifying and measuring the ways in which personalities differ is to be able to predict future behaviour, so as to anticipate or

## Box 20 Head Start programme

The Head Start programme, started in the USA in 1965 as an 8-week summer school, aimed to enhance the social and cognitive development of pre-school children through the provision of education, health, nutrition, and other social care services. Day-care centres operating throughout the school year were then set up specifically for the most disadvantaged children. Over 30 million children have participated in these programmes, and several attempts have been made to evaluate their impact. Results are mixed, but one consistent finding is that the programmes must be comprehensive and of significant duration. A few weeks of summer school is not sufficient to mitigate the effects of years of poverty. Some studies show that children who participate in Head Start score higher on IQ tests than comparable children, but the difference tends to 'fade' with time following the end of the programme, particularly for those who go on to poorer quality schools. Those who start the programme earlier (at the age of 3) show more benefit for longer than those who start later (at the age of 4). There is also some evidence of a broader range of benefits from Head Start than just enhancing IQ, such as being more likely to complete school, attend college, have higher earnings in their mid-20s, and being less likely to be involved in criminal activity or suffer from poor health as an adult.

modify it. However, measuring personality suffers from similar difficulties to those inherent in measuring intelligence because, like intelligence, there is no clear agreement about what personality is and it cannot be measured directly—it can only be inferred from the behaviours that are thought to reflect it.

Several theories of personality have been proposed and the main approaches are summarized in Table 2.

**Table 2 The main approaches to theories of personality**

| Approach | View of personality |
| --- | --- |
| Categorical type | People are fitted into broad categories, with each type being qualitatively different from others, e.g. type A or B; introvert or extrovert. |
| Trait | A descriptive approach in which people are defined according to how much of each of a list of traits they have, e.g. high conscientiousness; low introversion. |
| Behaviourist | Views personality as merely a reflection of the person's learning history—they repeat the responses that have been reinforced in the past. |
| Cognitive | Beliefs, thoughts, and mental processes are seen as primary in determining behaviour across situations. |
| Psychodynamic | Based on Freud's theory, personality is understood to be determined by intrapsychic structures (the id, ego, and superego), and by unconscious motives or conflicts from early childhood. |
| Individual | Emphasizes higher human motives and views personality as the individual's complete experience rather than as having separate parts. |
| Situational | Suggests that personality is not consistent but is merely a response to the situation. We learn to behave in ways that are appropriate to the situation through reinforcement. |
| Interactive | Combines the situational and trait approaches, so suggests that people have a tendency to behave in certain ways but that this is moderated by the demands of different situations. |

Each of the different approaches in Table 2 reflects a comprehensive theory and it is not possible to cover them in depth here. Instead we will highlight some of the main ways in which they differ, and we will use Eysenck's theory of personality, which combines elements of both the type and trait approaches, as an example.

Different theories of personality vary in the degree to which they see behaviours as determined by the individual or by the situations they are in, and in general, we tend to overestimate the importance of personality in explaining another's behaviour (*fundamental attribution error*). However, the situational and behavioural approaches may go too far when they suggest that all variation in behaviour is determined by situational factors or conditioned by patterns of reinforcement. If the situation or reinforcement contingencies accounted for everything then we would all behave identically in the same situation, which is clearly not so. Indeed, the situation may be influenced by internal events—different people may 'see' the same situations differently: if an acquaintance walks past someone without speaking, one person will see this as being ignored by an acquaintance whereas another will be thinking 'he didn't notice me'. Similarly, the nuance of the situation is important—a generally shy person may in fact be quite comfortable with public speaking (many actors say they are shy). So traits may not be consistent across all situations. Thus, most contemporary theories suggest that both situational and individual factors contribute to those relatively enduring and stable characteristics that we call 'personality'.

Approaches to personality also vary in the degree to which they see people as *types* or as having more or less of certain *traits*. Type theories tend to emphasize the similarities between people whereas trait approaches stress the differences between individuals and their inherent uniqueness. Eysenck's approach combines both: he used complex statistical techniques to analyse and group together the hundreds of traits shown by large numbers of people (e.g.

optimistic, aggressive, lazy). Initially he came up with two dimensions: introversion–extroversion and stability–neuroticism (emotionality), with the majority of people scoring in the middle of the dimensions. Each dimension is made up of a number of traits and someone who is high on one trait is thought likely to be high on the other traits in that dimension—giving an overall type. Eysenck's theory of personality is illustrated in Figure 15.

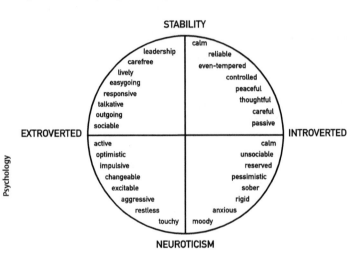

15. Eysenck's personality types

Eysenck proposed a biological basis to his theory, suggesting that these personality dimensions were related to differences in brain functioning. He suggested that extroverts have lower arousal levels and thus seek more stimulation and excitement than introverts. Twin studies have suggested a genetic component to introversion–extroversion and recent research into how the brain works has found some possible neural correlates (links to brain functioning). For example, extroversion has been linked to the network of brain systems controlling sensitivity to reward and generating approach behaviour. This may explain why extroversion is correlated with happiness since those high in extroversion will more easily feel the excitement of a potential reward. Similarly, extroversion is associated with enhanced allocation of attention in response to social stimuli, suggesting these may be more motivating for extroverts. In contrast, introverts' emotional centres in the brain are more easily activated by emotional stimuli, and introverts have more blood flow in the frontal lobes of their brain and in areas that deal with internal processes, such as planning and problem-solving. The discovery of neural correlates of personality suggests it has a biological basis, and that individual differences in personality are related to meaningful individual differences in brain structures and responses to social stimuli.

A psychological test has been developed to measure the dimensions of Eysenck's theory and it uses questions such as 'Do you like talking to people so much that you never miss the opportunity to talk to a stranger?' and 'Can you easily get some life into a dull party?' to indicate extroversion. Answering 'yes' to questions such as 'Do you often worry about things you shouldn't have done or said?' and 'Are you troubled by feelings of inferiority?' is taken to indicate greater neuroticism. Although many people view introversion and extroversion as categories, they actually reflect a single continuous dimension of personality on which a few score near either end and most fall in the middle. *Ambiversion* is the term used to describe those in the middle of the introversion–extroversion continuum who show some traits of both characteristics.

## What use are tests of intelligence and personality?

Scores on psychological tests measuring personality and intelligence supposedly help us to make predictions about behaviour and achievement. But the evidence suggests that neither personality nor intelligence is as fixed as the concept of psychometric testing suggests. There is evidence that some personality traits remain relatively stable over time, particularly after adolescence and early adulthood, but it is less clear that scores measuring them predict someone's actual behaviour in a given situation. This *consistency paradox* reflects the fact that we tend to see other people as being relatively consistent, as in 'John is the outgoing type', despite being unable to predict their actual behaviour at any one time. Examining behaviour across a range of situations shows that personality traits are more predictable at the general level (i.e. 'John is outgoing in most situations') but not so well in a single situation, as so many variables are involved, externally and internally, such as mood and fatigue.

There has also been much interest in whether IQ predicts behaviour. While there is a relationship between IQ and aspects of intelligent behaviour such as job performance, it is not a strong relationship and within most occupations there is a wide range of IQs. In fact, some studies suggest that socio-economic background is a better predictor of future academic and occupational success than IQ. A long-term study of children with very high IQs found that some became very successful adults but others did not, with no differences in IQ between the two groups. There were, however, great differences in motivation: the more successful individuals had much more ambition and drive to succeed.

Although psychologists have made significant advances in quantifying and measuring the differences between people, some caution is needed in using such information. In interpreting any single test score it is vital to remember that many factors may have influenced it, including genetic potential, experience, motivation, and conditions of testing. Thus, single scores such as those provided by an IQ test cannot be seen as defining the limit of a person's ability; rather they should be viewed as an indication of their current level or the approximate range within which they would generally fall. Other dangers associated with psychometric testing arise from value judgements about certain scores—for example, it may be implied that higher scores are better and that

Psychology

people who achieve them are 'superior'. In its most extreme form, this argument can be used for social and political purposes to support ideas such as eugenics which aims to improve the genetic composition of a population by promoting increased reproduction of more desired people/traits and reduced reproduction of less desired people/traits. But generally speaking, knowing more about how to measure the ways in which people differ according to dimensions such as intelligence and personality has helped us to understand more about the number of contributing variables, the potential for change, and the relationship to achievement and happiness.

# Chapter 8
# What happens when things go wrong? Abnormal psychology

Abnormal psychology is concerned with behaviour that is atypical or dysfunctional, and with mental disorder or disability. However, it is through understanding the processes involved in normal functioning (e.g. in perception, learning, memory, cognition, emotion, personality, development, and social relationships) that we can understand what happens when they go wrong. The study of illusions has revealed the degree to which, normally, we actively construct our notions of reality, and the enormous amount of brain activity that remains out of awareness (see Chapter 2). Yet we assume that we can know the real world and are not just hallucinating. How do we know? Why do we suppose that reality is normal and hallucinations are not, given that our knowledge of reality is the product of constructive processes, and therefore could itself be called illusory?

## How do we decide what is abnormal?

Extreme forms of psychological abnormality are easy to recognize, but the point at which normality becomes abnormality is much less clear. For example, it is normal to feel sad after a bereavement, but the lines between normal and abnormal grief, and between grief and clinical depression, are not so clear. It would be abnormal to keep every receipt you have ever been given, to the point where there is room for little else in your home, but is it also abnormal to keep most receipts for a year or two 'just in case'? Most people consider it normal to have occasional irrational fears, for example of heights or of public speaking, but what if the fear is severe enough to prevent you driving over bridges or doing your job? Our ideas about normality come from noticing the unusual or abnormal in the present, but they are also influenced by what happened in the past and by our sense of acceptability, by historical and cultural factors—think about changes in opinion about homosexuality, about its legal and psychiatric status, and arguments about parenting by two people of the same gender.

There are many ways of conceptualizing abnormality. *Psychological* ways emphasize personal distress and interference: if personal suffering is involved, or if the condition prevents someone achieving important goals, it is seen as dysfunctional and worthy of intervention. However, with this approach we struggle to account for people who lack insight into their difficulties, such as those with delusions of grandeur who are not distressed by believing that they are God, or those with anorexia who may view the advantages of being seriously underweight as outweighing the serious health risks. Similarly, defining behaviour (e.g. driving on the motorway) as abnormal solely on the grounds that it causes great distress may be problematic: the behaviour itself may be normal and it may be only the degree of distress that is abnormal.

*Medical conceptualizations* suggest abnormality is a symptom of an underlying disease (such as schizophrenia or manic depression), the cause of which may be genetic, or may involve structural or chemical abnormalities in the brain. This medical model has been criticized for ignoring the effects of the person's environment and social context, and for undermining personal responsibility, for example when people rely on a doctor for a 'cure'. Its validity has also been called into question because two people may have the same diagnosis, but different symptoms. Or they may not have enough symptoms to meet criteria for the diagnosis of a particular disease, but have one or two symptoms such as suspiciousness or social withdrawal at a severe level. Technically they do not have an 'illness', yet their behaviour may appear strikingly abnormal.

Abnormality has also been defined in terms of both *statistical* and *social norms*. So people are judged to have intellectual disability if their IQ is in the lowest 2.5 per cent of the population. However, this approach confounds normality with desirability. Desirable behaviours or attributes may be statistically uncommon but not seen as abnormal, such as having an IQ in the top 2.5 per cent! Furthermore, emotional problems such as depression or anxiety are sufficiently common to be statistically normal, and the context in which they occur helps to determine what would normally be expected: a degree of depression is a normal response to a relationship ending but not to winning the lottery. Behaviour that deviates from what is typical for the social context may also be seen as abnormal (undressing in a town centre or walking backwards down the street). Although this approach takes the person's environment into account, it is dependent upon prevailing social, moral, and cultural attitudes, and thus relies on value judgements about normality.

*Existential approaches* suggest abnormal behaviour is an inevitable response to an unpredictable world. Each person is responsible for defining their own normality (and identity), and disorder occurs when people feel compelled to conform to societal expectations instead of acting with authenticity in the pursuit of their own true values and goals. This can explain why someone's behaviour may be more of a problem for those around them, or for society, than for themselves (using non-prescribed drugs or smoking in a restaurant).

*Normalizing* or *health-based* approaches attempt to specify normality or healthy psychological functioning and then define abnormality in contrast to this. Ideal mental health is thought to involve characteristics such as accurate perception of reality; some degree of self-knowledge and awareness of one's feelings and motives; autonomy and confidence in the ability to exert self-control; a sense of self-worth and self-acceptance; the ability to form close and satisfying relationships; and environmental mastery—being able to meet the varying demands of day-to-day situations. Clearly not everyone will meet this ideal all the time, and one difficulty for this approach is deciding how big a deviation has to be before it is considered to be abnormal.

As none of the definitions above is completely satisfactory, it may be better to combine various elements of them, as shown in Box 21.

### Box 21 Factors which may indicate that behaviour is abnormal

None of these features is necessary or sufficient for behaviour to be seen as abnormal, but they can indicate abnormality:

- suffering
- irrationality and incomprehensibility
- unpredictability and loss of control
- personal and social maladaptiveness
- unconventionality
- violation of moral or idealized standards
- causing distress to others observing the behaviour.

This combined approach is flexible, but based on subjective judgements about which people may disagree.

Part of the difficulty in defining abnormality is that each person's history as well as their current situation contributes to the way they think, feel, and act (behave), and this should be taken into account. For instance, a particular behaviour may have reflected an adaptive response in an earlier environment. A child who learns to avoid punishment or criticism by keeping quiet may be showing behaviour that is functional in those circumstances. However, if the reticence persists into adulthood, then it may prevent that person forming close and confiding relationships. The process here may be normal, and initially adaptive, but it may result later in behaviour which is maladaptive, interfering with the ability to relate well to others, and causes distress.

## Classifying abnormality

There are advantages and disadvantages inherent in attempting to classify the different forms of abnormal behaviour. One potential advantage is that, if different types of abnormality have different causes, then we may be able to understand more about the various syndromes by studying a number of people with a specific problem and looking for similarities, for instance in their history, behaviour, or physiology. By studying many people who had panic attacks it was noticed that they tended to interpret their bodily sensations during an attack as signs of impending catastrophe: breathlessness was taken as a sign of impending suffocation; a pounding heart suggested imminent heart attack. Further research has shown that these catastrophic interpretations play a central role in panic attacks.

Classifying and labelling different types of abnormal behaviour into *diagnoses*, the medical names for disorders (e.g. *anorexia nervosa* or *hypochondriasis*), conveys a wealth of information in relatively few words. For example, the agreed criteria for the definition tell us that people with anorexia over-emphasize the importance of shape and weight and restrict their intake in order to become thinner. Information gathered from well conducted research on the treatment of anorexia also helps to work out which treatments are likely to be effective. But when using diagnostic labels it is important to avoid stereotyping. The danger is that once people are given a label, they may be seen as identical to other people with the same label when in fact the differences are as marked as the similarities. This can mean that important details about *their* problem and personal responses (or additional difficulties such as low self-esteem) are ignored. It can also be dehumanizing when the person rather than the illness is labelled, as in 'he's a schizophrenic' rather than 'he is suffering from schizophrenia', as if the person is defined by the illness and is not otherwise a person.

Psychiatric diagnoses are made according to detailed classification systems such as those presented in the *Diagnostic and Statistical Manual of Mental Disorders*, which is produced by the American Psychiatric Association. Such systems, even though they are constantly being revised (as for the 5th edition in 2013), are useful for research and for clinical purposes. They provide a 'shared language' for understanding each disorder to people working in different places, so that they know that they are referring to the same thing. They also provide a clearly defined way of ascertaining whether the criteria for assigning a diagnosis are met. The main categories of abnormal behaviour covered in DSM-IV-TR are shown in Table 3.

To meet the criteria for diagnosis according to the DSM the person must have been experiencing a minimum number of the specified symptoms for a certain period of time, and those symptoms must cause significant distress or impairment in functioning. So these are not 'all or none' definitions and the different forms of abnormal behaviour exist on a continuum with normal behaviour. Thus, it is easy to

**Table 3  Different types of abnormal behaviour**

| Category | Examples of specific disorders |
|---|---|
| Schizophrenic and other psychotic disorders | A group of disorders characterized by symptoms of loss of contact with reality as in hallucinations or delusions, marked disturbances of thought and perception, disorganized and bizarre behaviour, and negative symptoms such as a lack of emotional response and low motivation. |
| Anxiety disorders | Several disorders, including *post-traumatic stress disorder*, in which the main symptoms are of anxiety either in response to a particular stimulus as in *phobias*, or more diffuse anxiety as in *generalized anxiety*. Many anxiety disorders include the experience of panic attacks, defined in terms of the sudden and intense onset of anxiety symptoms. |
| Mood disorders | Disturbances of normal mood ranging from extreme depression to abnormal elation *(mania)*, or alternating between the two *(bipolar disorder)*. |
| Somatoform disorders | Physical symptoms, such as pain or paralysis, for which no physical basis can be found, and in which psychological factors appear to play a role (e.g. paralysis that is apparent in some situations but not in others). Also included in this category are *hypochondriasis*, *somatization disorder*, and *body dysmorphic disorder* (preoccupation with a perceived defect in appearance). |
| Dissociative disorders | Disruption in the usually integrated functions of consciousness, memory, identity, or perception for emotional reasons. Included in this category are *dissociative identity disorder* (formerly *multiple personality disorder*), *depersonalization disorder*, and *dissociative amnesia* and *fugue* (e.g. being unable to recall a traumatic experience). |

Psychology

| | |
|---|---|
| Sexual and gender identity disorders | Sexual desire and sexual preference disorders such as sexual interest in children (*paedophilia*), or in objects (*fetishism*), gender identity disorders such as *transsexualism* (feeling that you are trapped in a body of the wrong gender), and sexual arousal disorders (e.g. impotence). |
| Eating disorders | Severe disturbances in eating behaviour (e.g. *binge eating disorder, anorexia*, and *bulimia nervosa*). |
| Sleep disorders | Abnormalities in the amount, quality, or timing of sleep (e.g. *insomnia*), or abnormal behaviour or physiological events occurring during sleep (e.g. nightmares, night terrors, sleepwalking). |
| Impulse control disorders not elsewhere classified | Failure to resist an impulse, drive, or temptation that may harm oneself or others, e.g. *kleptomania* involving impulsive stealing for no personal gain, or *trichotillomania* involving habitual pulling out of one's hair, or *pathological gambling*. |
| Personality disorders | Enduring patterns of inner experience and behaviour that are pervasive and inflexible, lead to distress or impairment, and deviate from social norms, e.g. *narcissistic personality disorder* involves a pattern of grandiosity, need for admiration, and lack of empathy; *obsessive-compulsive personality* is characterized by preoccupation with orderliness, perfectionism, and control. |
| Substance-related disorders | *Substance use disorders*, such as excessive use of or dependence on alcohol or drugs, and *substance induced disorders* where the use of substances leads to other symptoms such as psychosis or delirium. |
| Factitious disorders | Symptoms that are intentionally produced or feigned in order to assume a 'sick role', to gain financial benefits or reduce responsibility. This is usually self-inflicted but can be acted out against someone else, usually a dependent child (*factitious disorder by proxy*) |

recognize oneself in reading about abnormal behaviour, and people may feel that they have every diagnosis in the book when they first read the details.

## Explaining abnormality and developing effective treatments

Historically abnormalities have been attributed to a wide variety of causes, from dietary deficiencies to the phases of the moon or evil spirits. More recently scientific methods such as careful observation and hypothesis testing have led to numerous theories. Not surprisingly, these explanations are quite closely related to the different views of personality that are outlined in Chapter 7. Explanations of abnormal behaviour vary in the degree to which they focus on the past or present, whether they are based on psychological theory or medical models, and on whether the views of the therapist and patient are given equal weight. They also advocate different types of intervention or treatment.

The *medical model*, which dominated psychiatry for many years, understood abnormal behaviour to result from physical or mental illnesses caused by genetic, biochemical, or physical dysfunctions in the brain or body. One of the early successes of the medical model was the discovery that *general paresis*, a debilitating form of dementia that was common in the early 20th century, was a long-term consequence of infection with syphilis. As in other branches of medicine, the priority in practice is to establish the correct diagnosis. Treatment follows from this and is often a physical intervention aimed at altering brain functioning, such as medication (e.g. anti-depressant or anti-psychotic drugs), psychosurgery (surgical techniques to destroy or disconnect specific areas of the brain), or ECT (electroconvulsive therapy which induces seizures that affect the balance of chemicals in the brain). Both psychosurgery and ECT were widely and relatively indiscriminately used before the advent of drug therapies. They are now used mostly as a last resort when other treatments have failed and urgent intervention is needed (e.g. due to high risk of suicide). New treatments are still being developed: research suggests that it may become possible to relieve treatment-resistant depression using highly specific methods of deep brain stimulation. Pharmacotherapy research continues to produce new drugs that have increasingly specific effects. However, so far these do not work for everyone, and relapse is common following discontinuation of medication. While modern psychoactive medications may not have the debilitating side effects of earlier ones, effects such as weight gain, joint stiffness, and, occasionally, increases in suicidality or aggression still occur.

*Psychodynamic approaches* were based originally on the theories of Sigmund Freud and explain abnormality in terms of conflicts between instinctual drives, leading to anxieties. These conflicts are dealt with by *defence mechanisms*, or strategies used to avoid or reduce the experience of anxiety, and to protect the person's ego. Treatment often focuses on early life experiences and involves helping to reveal the patient's unconscious motives and to resolve the original conflicts. Psychodynamic therapists developed techniques such as *free association*, encouraging patients to say whatever comes into their minds, and then interpreting the associations in terms of psychodynamic theories.

*Humanistic psychotherapy* focuses rather on the present, and views patients as being in the best position to understand their own problems. Each person's sense of self is seen as critical in promoting personal growth and well-being, and the aim of therapy is to promote self-esteem and self-acceptance. Therapists adopt an attitude of 'unconditional positive regard': that is, being genuinely non-judgemental, warm, accepting, and empathic—attitudes subsequently widely recommended.

Purely behavioural approaches explained psychological symptoms as maladaptive behaviour patterns which were learnt and could thus be unlearnt. Initially they claimed that it was not necessary to understand the origins of abnormal behaviour in order to treat it, and interventions focused entirely on the present, on observable behaviour. Internal events and meanings, and the patient's history were considered unimportant. Therapy techniques included reconditioning by, for example, *systematic desensitization*, in which relaxation techniques are used to reduce anxiety during exposure to a hierarchy of increasingly anxiety-provoking situations.

More recently, behavioural approaches have been combined with cognitive approaches to form cognitive-behavioural therapy (CBT). Cognitive-behavioural approaches take into account history, current patterns of behaviour, findings from experimental research in cognitive psychology and from research into clinical effectiveness, and above all *cognition*. Cognition includes thoughts, assumptions, beliefs, attitudes, expectations, and so on: reflections of all the ways in which someone makes sense of the past, present, and future, and which may be reflected in dreams and images as well as in behaviour. Patients are encouraged to examine the cognitive processes by which they arrive at a particular state of mind, and to change these processes together with the behaviours that may reinforce them so as to feel better.

In all the main psychotherapies the precise intervention used depends on the patient's idiosyncratic 'formulation': i.e. on the way in which the theory is applied to the problems experienced by the patient in practice. The formulation is intended to provide a personalized understanding of relevant factors. Using an example from CBT, these would include past experiences, vulnerability to psychological disorder, precipitants of problems, and the factors maintaining the problem in the current environment. So someone bullied at school might develop beliefs about being unacceptable to others. Such beliefs leave them vulnerable to feeling inadequate or unlikeable as adults and when activated by environmental circumstances (e.g. a rejection experience) these beliefs prompt maladaptive patterns of responding (such as avoidance or self-protective strategies) that maintain the problem. A cycle of maintenance might start with thoughts about being unlikeable, leading to anxiety about social situations, and avoidance of social contact. Resulting isolation then confirms the belief in being unlikeable. Interventions include re-evaluating the validity of thoughts and testing these out in the patient's current circumstances using a combination of cognitive and behavioural methods. These are described in an introductory book by Westbrook. (See Figure 16). This method can also be applied issues arising from the past and reflected in current beliefs.

Recent research has shown that children who have been bullied between the ages of 8 and 10 are seven times more likely than others to have symptoms of enduring psychological problems at the age of 12. In this study both the bullied children and those who were not bullied had similar degrees of family adversity, previous psychological problems, and adverse experiences of parenting. Such research illustrates well the links between academic research and clinical practice. Results contribute to the understanding of the problem and of its development and stimulate work on developing effective treatments.

There are many forms of cognitive-behavioural interventions and recent innovations include developments in the ways in which CBT interventions are administered, including self-help packages or computer programmes that teach people to challenge their thinking or to experiment with new, functional ways of behaving. Developments in the theory underlying CBT suggest that as much can be gained by changing the way we relate to our thoughts as by changing the content of our thinking. Hence, meditation techniques have been integrated with elements of CBT to form mindfulness-based cognitive therapy (MBCT) which has been shown to be effective in preventing relapse in those who have had recurrent episodes of depression. Techniques for changing styles of thinking (cognitive biases), such as cognitive bias modification, are also being researched outside the clinic.

16. **CBT: Finding another way of seeing things.** 'The wind was against them now, and Piglet's ears streamed behind him like banners as he fought his way along, and it seemed hours before he got them into the shelter of the Hundred Acre Wood and they stood up straight again, to listen, a little nervously, to the roaring of the gale among the tree tops. 'Supposing a tree fell down, Pooh, when we were underneath it?' 'Supposing it didn't,' said Pooh after careful thought

In summary, attempting to differentiate abnormal from normal behaviour is not straightforward: what is considered abnormal depends on the context, on current values and norms, and on the ways in which normality and abnormality are conceptualized. Different ways of understanding normal personality and normal behaviour will also influence how abnormality is understood and treated. Many factors contribute to causing psychological problems, including genetics, brain structure and chemistry, early experiences, learning history, unconscious conflicts, recent stressful or traumatic events, and thinking styles. Classification systems such as DSM aid communication and understanding, but their reliability and validity are still being questioned.

Despite these difficulties, abnormal psychology has contributed much to the development of effective interventions. In considering which treatment is best it is difficult to compare their efficacy accurately as they are not all equally amenable to testing. How do we measure the degree of unconscious conflict? The most demonstrably effective treatments are those like CBT that are based on testable theories and that have been evaluated using scientific methods: independent 'blind' assessment of effects, experiments designed to test specific hypotheses, multiple standardized measurement of outcome, long-term follow-up, and appropriate comparison groups. At present, there is evidence that both psychological and drug treatments can be effective in ameliorating distressing symptoms, and psychological treatments such as CBT may have an advantage over drug treatments in terms of lower *relapse rates* (the proportion of people who deteriorate or relapse once treatment has finished). However, the effectiveness of all interventions varies according to the individual's presentation. Some conditions are more 'treatable' than others, and factors such as the duration and severity of a problem affect the success of treatment (drug treatments are more indicated for severe depression than mild depression). Alternatively, some presentations will warrant combined drug and psychological interventions, and there is a useful summary of current practical guidelines in a book called *What Works for Whom*, written jointly by a psychiatrist and a psychologist. It has been possible for abnormal psychology to develop in the way that it has partly because of advances made in other areas of psychology. Examples include understanding the ways in which perception and attention are influenced by moods (how being fearful keeps one on the lookout for dangers or *hypervigilant*); how one might be able to detect a signal without being aware of doing so, and become distressed without understanding why; how memories can be inaccurate as well as accurate; and how hard it can be to withstand the pressure of a peer group. A long series of experiments carried out with students in their first weeks at university has shown that writing about previous traumatic experiences for two 15 minute periods, and some while after the actual event, is associated with better mental and physical health, and with better degree results three years later. This occurs even if no one ever reads what has been written or speaks to the students personally about those events. Why? The research continues.

Thinking again about the hallucinations mentioned at the start of this chapter, research by cognitive-neuroscientists suggests that these might arise from a disturbance in perceptual processes that interferes with the ability to separate considerations of experience and belief. Hallucinations might occur when error-dependent updating of inferences and beliefs about the world no longer functions as it should (using the Bayesian inference described in Chapter 2). The details of such hypotheses are too complex to be fully elaborated here. The point is that exploring the variables responsible for effects such as these can contribute to understanding what has happened when things go wrong, and potentially also to the development of new treatments. Future developments in abnormal psychology, whether they are directed towards improving treatments or preventing problems arising, will therefore not take place in isolation, and the ways in which they are applied will need to be subjected to similarly rigorous scientific and ethical standards.

# Chapter 9
# How do we influence each other? Social psychology

Social interaction plays a crucial role in human evolution, in development, and in everyday social life, so there are numerous areas of social psychology to explore, such as group dynamics, bystander intervention, behaviour of crowds, impression formation, the psychology of cheating and deceit, and of social behaviour. The text books by Hogg and Vaughan and by Kassin, Fein, and Markus are good sources. It is clear that we must have a 'social brain', but the mechanisms involved in understanding the mental state of others (their feelings, thoughts, intentions, and actions) are not yet fully understood. Cognitive-neuroscientists studying social interaction in the relatively new field of social neuroscience are still developing research paradigms to allow analysis of brain activity during the reciprocal interplay between people. The assumption is that the computations made in the brain during social interactions will resemble those made during basic cognitive and emotional processes, combined in a manner specific to social interaction.

Studies have produced some intriguing results. For example, cells have been observed in monkeys and birds which fire both when an animal acts and when the animal observes the same action performed by another animal, and brain activity consistent with this has been observed in humans. These could be part of a 'Mirror Neuron System' specialized for understanding the behaviour of others: activity in these cells could help us to engage with their emotions and allow us to grasp their intentions. Similarly, imitating an action, as even newborn babies do (e.g. when an adult sticks out their tongue), allows the possibility of experiencing something like the feelings, intentions, and sensations of someone else.

Before such work became possible, social behaviour, and the ways in which we influence each other, was studied at a very different level, exploring indirect as well as direct influences. You do not need a social psychologist to tell you that people do things when alone that they would not dream of doing in public, or behave quite differently in the company of friends than they would with colleagues. This impact on human behaviour of the presence of others has been called *social facilitation* due to the initial observations that the presence of others enhanced performance on simple tasks. One obvious form of social facilitation is competition: in general, performance is enhanced if people believe that they are competing with others—even if there is no prize. It seems that the mere presence of others, rather than the atmosphere of competition, is the crucial element. Even when people are asked not to compete, they work faster when they can see others working (the *coaction effect*), or when they are being observed by others (the *audience effect*).

Experiments have shown that social facilitation can be produced by simply telling the person that others are performing the same task elsewhere. Hence, your motivation to study may be increased by hearing that a classmate is already hard at it. Social facilitation has been demonstrated in animals too—even cockroaches run faster when they are being watched by their peers!

More direct forms of social influence involve attempting to change the behaviour of others. This happens when someone tries to influence the group as a whole (*leadership*), when several group members encourage others to adopt a particular attitude *(conformity)*, when an authority figure tries to achieve compliance to their demands *(obedience)*, or when the attitudes of one group influence behaviour towards another group *(prejudice)*. This chapter focuses on these four types of behaviour.

## A born leader?

It was originally thought that leadership was a trait that some people possessed and others did not: hence the term, 'a born leader'. A number of attributes, such as height, weight, intelligence, confidence, and charisma, have been proposed as being related to leadership, though none of them consistently distinguishes leaders from non-leaders. Even intelligence is only slightly higher in typical leaders than in the average group member, and we can all think of leaders who are not particularly charismatic—so psychologists have explored other possibilities.

First, leadership style has been shown to influence the behaviour and productivity of group members. In general, a participative style, which attempts to involve all in decision-making, promotes high productivity with good relationships between group members. A more authoritarian, directive style allows group members less say in decisions and produces equal productivity (provided the leader is present), but tends to lead to poorer relationships and less cooperation. Laissez-faire leadership, which leaves the group to its own devices, results in lower productivity. The results of these studies have influenced the development of management strategies which encourage a move away from authoritarian models towards the more egalitarian process of allowing workers to have a say in the running of the organization.

Research on the situational aspects of leadership suggests that leadership is primarily determined by the functions that the group needs a leader to fulfil, and there is some evidence to support this notion. For example, more directive, task-oriented leadership produces greater benefits when conditions are more extreme (either favourable or unfavourable). This may help to explain the frequency of dictators as leaders in countries that are experiencing times of extreme hardship (e.g. Hitler's ascendancy during the 1930s). To find out more about situational influences on leadership, psychologists have studied the effects of putting a random person in a central position. Experiments have shown that if members of a group are forced to communicate only through one central person, then that person begins to function as a leader: sending more messages, solving problems faster, making fewer errors, and becoming more satisfied with the efforts made. People put in positions of leadership tend to accept the challenge, behave like leaders, and be recognized by others as leaders. This may explain why people who do not appear to be natural leaders can nevertheless rise to the occasion.

## Conformity

Understanding leadership helps to explain the effect of an individual on a group, but the effects of a group on an individual are also of interest. You may have noticed that if several people have already given the same answer to a question, the last person is unlikely to disagree—and a 'hung jury' is a fairly rare occurrence. *Conformity* is the act of matching attitudes, beliefs, and behaviours to (perceived) group norms. Conformity is often associated with youth culture (e.g. conforming to a particular hair or dress style), but actually affects all ages and there are obvious benefits to society of conforming to group norms (helping vulnerable adults or children; or waiting in line). Early investigations of the human desire to agree with the majority view found that over time an individual's opinions tended to fall into line with it, particularly in situations that were ambiguous. It was suggested that this reflects how social norms develop to provide a common frame of reference.

Solomon Asch furthered this work by asking people to pick which of three lines was the same length as a given example (see Figure 17).

The group included stooges (instructed to give the same wrong answer in 12 of the 18 trials). The results showed that most of the participants conformed at least some of the time and on average people conformed to the wrong answer a third of the time. Subsequent experiments showed that the degree of conformity was influenced by the ambiguity of the task (when the correct answer was less obvious conformity increased) and by the unanimity of the group. The dissent of even one person reduced conformity.

There are different levels of conformity. In Asch's experiments it turned out that some of those who conformed knew they were giving the wrong answer but did so because they didn't want to disagree, they feared social disapproval, or they feared that they would mess up the experiment. This level of conformity is also called *compliance* (going along with the majority opinion even though you don't personally agree with it). As one might expect rates of hand-washing after going to the toilet are lower when people believe they are not being observed as sometimes people are complying rather than internalizing the value. In contrast, deeper levels of conformity, also called *identification* or *internalization*, involve taking on board the opinions of another (a celebrity) or of a group (a school or a management team). This is strongest when the source is perceived to be expert, or at least credible, and when the task is difficult and urgent—in a crisis or emergency we will do whatever the doctor says. Indeed, levels of conformity vary according to many factors, including gender, culture, and situational factors (such as whether we are observed, task difficulty, how important we perceive it to be to be accurate or truthful, how well we know the others in the group, and how much we value their opinions).

## Obedience

Complying with the demands of an authority figure is called *obedience*, and scientific investigations of it were originally

(a)

(b)

(c)

prompted by atrocities committed during wars, such as the Holocaust or the killing of Vietnamese civilians at My Lai. After these wars it became apparent that many soldiers, who appeared to be ordinary decent people, had committed atrocious, illegal acts. When asked why they had done these things, a common defence was 'I was following orders'. Psychologists investigating obedience looked at just how far the average person will go, simply because they are told to do so. Box 22 describes a famous experiment investigating obedience in the general public, which is illustrated in Figure 18.

Many aspects of civilized life, such as the legal, military, and school systems, rely on people obeying the instructions of authority figures, and it has even been suggested that obedience to authority is vital for communal life and may have been built into our genetic make-up during evolution. However, psychological factors also play a part. For example, in Milgram's experiments, politeness conventions may have made it difficult for the participants to refuse to continue once they had started, or refusing to continue may have meant admitting that giving painful shocks to others was wrong and suggest that they disapproved of the experimenter. This makes it easier to understand why so few people disobey orders during war, when punishments for disobedience are more serious.

17. **Resistance to majority opinion**

(a) All of the group members except the man sixth from the left are confederates instructed to give uniformly wrong answers on 12 of the 18 trials. No. 6, who has been told he is participating in an experiment in visual judgement, therefore finds himself a lone dissenter when he gives the correct answers
(b) The participant, showing the strain of repeated disagreement with the majority, leans forward anxiously to look at the test materials
(c) Unusually, this participant persists in his opinion, saying that 'he has to call them as he sees them'

## Box 22 Extremes of obedience

Members of the public were recruited to participate in 'a study of memory'. Participants were told that they would play the role of 'teacher' and would be teaching a series of word pairs to a 'learner'. Teachers were instructed to press a lever to deliver an electric shock to the learner for every error made. Teachers saw learners being strapped into an electrically wired chair with an electrode placed on their wrist, and being given a sample shock of 45 volts to convince them of the generator's authenticity. Then, seated in front of the generator with 30 switches ranging from '15 volts—Mild shock'—to '450 volts—Danger: Severe shock', teachers were told to move up a level for each error made. The experimenter remained in the room throughout. The learner was an actor who did not receive shocks but who had been trained to respond as if he had, and briefed to make many errors. As the shocks became stronger, the actor began to shout and swear. At the level marked 'Extreme intensity shock' the actor went quiet and stopped responding to questions. Not surprisingly, many participants objected and asked to stop the experiment. The experimenter simply instructed them to continue. A staggering 65 per cent continued right to the end of the shock series (450 volts), and none stopped before 300 volts (when the actor began to kick the adjoining wall). The results of this experiment suggested that ordinary people will go very far indeed when they are instructed to do so by someone perceived to be in a position of authority.

The presence of the experimenter increased obedience: when instructions were issued by telephone obedience dropped from 65 to 21 per cent and several participants cheated by giving weaker shocks.

Milgram (1974).

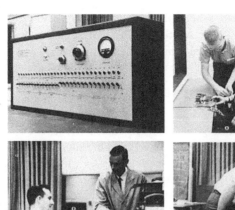

18. Milgram's experiment on obedience. Top left: The 'shock generator'. Top right: The victim is strapped into the 'electric chair'. Bottom left: A subject receives the sample shock before starting the 'teaching session'. Bottom right: Unusually, this subject refuses to go on with the experiment

Two other factors, which are also relevant to the obedience seen during wars, affected obedience in these experiments. First, people are more prepared to inflict pain if they can distance themselves from the victim—where the 'teacher' had to force the 'learner's' hand down onto a shock plate obedience was much lower than when not required to see or touch the 'learner'. This has parallels with modern weapons which can be fired at the touch of a button at an invisible enemy, causing invisible suffering. Indeed, it may be psychologically easier at the time to kill millions with a nuclear missile than to kill one person face-to-face. Second, believing the violence to be a means to an end in a worthy cause, or to have *ideological justification*, increases obedience both in the laboratory and in a war zone. In the experiments, participants believed that they were contributing to scientific research. When the experiment was repeated without the associations of a prestigious university, obedience rates dropped.

## Prejudice

Social psychology is also concerned with interactions between groups, and psychologists have suggested that dividing people into ethnic groups, and stereotyping behaviour according to group membership may have had evolutionary advantages. Indeed brain imaging studies showed greater amygdala activation in the response of Caucasians to black faces, and this correlated with prejudiced attitudes—but only for unknown black faces, not for familiar black faces. One hypothesis is that stereotyping according to racial groups may originally have been a primitive method of threat detection. Box 23 describes one of the many experiments that have investigated how belonging to a particular group can change behaviour.

Despite its artificiality, this experiment has many implications for prejudice in the real world. Prejudices are relatively enduring (usually negative) attitudes about a group (the *outgroup*) that are extended towards all members of that group. Prejudice often involves *stereotyping*—that is, the tendency to categorize people according to some readily identifiable characteristic such as age, race, sex, or occupation, and then to attribute to the individual the characteristics that are supposedly typical of members of that group. For example, someone who is prejudiced against women may believe that women are stupid and weak, and they will apply this belief to every woman they encounter. While the stereotypes involved in prejudices may contain a grain of truth (for example, on average women are physically weaker than men), they are frequently overly general: some women are stronger than some men; overly rigid: not all women are weak or stupid; or simply inaccurate: there is no evidence that women are less intelligent than men.

## Box 23 Are blue or brown eyes better?

Some 8-year-old children were invited by their teacher (Jane Elliott) to take part in an exercise that would help them better understand racism. She told them that those with brown eyes were more intelligent and 'better' people than those with blue eyes. She then gave the 'brownies' special privileges such as extra helpings at lunch and extra play time, and denigrated the 'blueys' by saying that they were less intelligent, dirty, shifty, and lazy. Blueys were made to wear a special collar so they could be easily identified. Behaviour in both groups changed: the blueys showed signs of lowered self-esteem and depressed mood, and did less well in their work, while the brownies became critical and oppressive towards their 'inferiors'.

After a few days, the teacher said that she had made a mistake, and the blueys were in fact the superior ones, and the behaviour patterns reversed (although to a lesser degree).

Of course, the exercise and its real aim were fully explained to the children once the study was over.

Aronson and Osherow (1980).

Prejudice is a global phenomenon and clearly situational influences contribute to its development. The blue eyes/brown eyes experiment suggests that prejudice can be created by giving one group privileges over another, and other studies show that even just arbitrarily allocating people to groups leads to people favouring those in their own (*ingroup*) group and discriminating against those in the outgroup. Another suggestion is that prejudice develops when groups perceive themselves to be in competition for the same limited resources. This was tested in a field experiment at a summer camp called Robbers' Cave (see Box 24).

## Box 24 Robbers' cave experiment

Twenty-two 11–12-year-old boys participated in this study of cooperative behaviour at a summer camp (Robbers' Cave).

*Stage 1*: The boys were allocated to one of two groups without knowing of each other's existence. Each group chose a name and formed a group identity by cooperating on tasks and wearing caps and t-shirts showing the group's name. Each group developed group norms for behaviour such as swimming naked or not mentioning homesickness.

*Stage 2*: Friction was introduced by allowing the groups to become aware of each other and having them compete for prizes in a grand tournament. Conflict quickly developed, together with negative attitudes (prejudices) towards each other, fighting between the groups, and stealing or damaging possessions.

*Stage 3*: Cooperative activities were introduced to reduce conflict. Equal status contact alone was not enough. Identifying goals that both groups wanted but could only be achieved through between-group cooperation—for example, pooling funds to rent a movie or pulling together to free a truck—was far more effective. Such cooperative activities succeeded in eliminating prejudices.

The researchers concluded that contact alone is insufficient to eliminate prejudice—it needed to be accompanied by the presence of superordinate goals that promote united, cooperative action.

Sherif, Harvey, White, Hood, and Sherif (1961).

Group conflict theory offers an explanation for negative attitudes towards racial integration and efforts to promote diversity—the majority group perceives the minority group(s) to be in competition with the majority group for resources, power, and prestige. This theory also helps to explain patterns of discrimination. For example, cross-cultural studies show that escalation in violence between groups is linked to shortages in resources. Then groups may attempt to remove the source of competition by limiting the opportunities of the outgroup (e.g. through active discrimination) or by decreasing their proximity to the outgroup (e.g. by denying immigrant access).

However, factors other than those that are situational also influence the development of prejudices. Personality characteristics, such as being less flexible and more authoritarian, are associated with prejudice, which may help to explain why two people who have had similar experiences can have differing levels of prejudice, and why those who show one prejudice are more likely to have other prejudices too. Prejudice can also arise from a general need to see oneself positively: people come to see any groups to which they belong more positively than other groups and then develop positive prejudices about their own groups and negative prejudices about others (*ethnocentrism*). Prejudice can also be a form of *scapegoating*, in which aggression is directed towards an innocent third party (usually seen by the aggressor(s) as a legitimate target) because it is not possible to direct aggression toward the real target—who may for instance be too dangerous or inaccessible.

It used to be thought that increased contact and decreased segregation would help to reduce prejudice. The absence of direct contact with another group leads to *autistic hostility* (ignorance of others), which produces a failure to understand the reasons for their actions, and provides no opportunities to find out if negative interpretations of their behaviour are incorrect. Thus, contact between opposing groups is needed before prejudices can be reduced, provided that contact does not reinforce stereotypes or inequities, as when male bosses employ female secretaries or cleaners. Furthermore, because inequity and competition for scarce resources facilitate the development of prejudice, contact to reduce prejudice should be based on equality (equal status contact), and encourage the pursuit of common goals rather than competition. Research investigating intergroup conflict in many countries (e.g. Northern Ireland and South Africa) suggests that contact works best when group memberships remain salient, and positive exemplars of outgroups cannot be explained away as 'exceptions to the rule' who happen to disconfirm stereotypes. In addition, contact that facilitates friendship, self-disclosure, and sharing of personal information, and even having friends of friends in the outgroup, help to reduce prejudice.

The processes involved in social facilitation, leadership, conformity, obedience, and prejudice show that our thoughts, feelings, and behaviours are influenced by others. Recent work in social psychology, even if we are only just beginning to unravel the details of what is going on in the brain, also shows that our social behaviour is influenced by the constant automatic reaction to and interpretation of our environments. For example, being exposed to words relating to hostility, even so briefly that it is outside conscious awareness, leads to more negative attitudes.

The practical applications of research into social psychology are vast. Studies of social facilitation and leadership show that working conditions impact on productivity and satisfaction. Studies of obedience and conformity show that we are much more likely to be influenced by pressure from others than we realize, and they provide a framework for understanding why we are susceptible to such pressures. Greater understanding of the factors contributing to obedience and conformity has been useful both in situations where conformity and obedience are desirable, such as in the military, and in situations where it is important that people stay true to their own opinions. For example, research suggests that juries of six or seven rather than of 12 may be more effective, as smaller groups are less likely to produce undue pressure to conform and larger groups tend to be dominated by a few strong characters. The psychological study of prejudice has facilitated the development of more effective programmes to reduce prejudice and conflict between groups.

There are many interesting areas of social psychology that we have not been able to cover here, such as group dynamics, bystander intervention, behaviour of crowds, impression formation, the psychology of cheating and deceit, interpersonal attraction, and the psychology of social networking and Internet behaviour. Both antisocial behaviour, such as cyber-bullying, rioting, terrorism, and hooliganism, and pro-social behaviour, such as acts of altruism, are of interest. The major challenges for the future are to find out more about the many factors that help to predict, control, or modify both types of behaviour, and to discover more about the cognitive neuroscience of social interaction.

# Chapter 10
# What is psychology for?

As well as being an academic discipline, psychology has many practical uses. Academic research helps us to understand, explain, predict, or modify what goes on in the mind: the control centre for cognition, affect, and behaviour (what we think, feel, and do). It also contributes to the development of theories and hypotheses to test, and to stimulating original research in applied settings, so that developments in the academic and professional fields can influence each other, with especially productive results when communication between them is good. Kahneman's work (Chapter 4) provides a good example. Experimental studies of the processes involved in thinking and reasoning revealed the biases that influence the judgements we make, and these ideas underpin the new field of behavioural economics. But they have also been used in medical diagnosis, legal judgements, intelligence analysis, philosophy, finance, statistics, and military strategy. Equally, the observations of professional psychologists may stimulate academic interest. For example, psychologists working in clinics noticed that patients with health anxiety (hyperchondriasis) often spent long periods looking up health-related information on the Internet. This led to experimental investigation of 'cyberchondria', which finds that Internet searching does indeed fuel anxiety about health. Similarly, observations of young people's use of the numerous products of information technology has led to explorations of their effects on social relationships, on language use, and on the brain—just to begin with. Research in these areas is developing fast.

## Where do professional psychologists work?

Psychologists are interested in mental functioning in both humans and animals, across a range of settings, hence they work in numerous different places as applied or professional psychologists. Clinical or health psychologists usually work in health care settings such as hospitals, clinics, GP practices, or in private practices. Clinical psychologists mainly use psychological techniques to help people overcome difficulties and distress. They deliver and evaluate therapy and other interventions, and use their research skills to develop new techniques and methods: to teach and supervise others, and to contribute to the planning, development, and management of services generally. Health psychologists are more concerned with the psychological aspects of their patients' physical health, and apply their knowledge to aid the treatment or prevention of illness and disability. For example, devising education and prevention programmes about AIDS or diet; finding out about how best to communicate with patients and help them adhere to treatment plans, or helping people to manage chronic health-related problems such as diabetes.

Professional psychologists also work outside health care settings. For example, forensic psychologists work with prison, probation, or police services, and use their skills in helping to solve crimes, predict the behaviour of offenders or suspects, and in rehabilitating offenders. Educational psychologists specialize in all aspects of children's education, such as assessing learning disabilities (e.g. dyslexia) and developing plans to maximize learning. Environmental psychologists are interested in the interactions between people and their environment, and work in areas such as town planning, ergonomics, and designing housing so as to reduce crime or offices to maximize performance at work. Sports psychologists try to help athletes maximize their performance, and develop training schemes and ways of dealing with the stresses of competition.

Many areas of business also utilize professional psychologists. Occupational psychologists consider all aspects of working life, including selection, training, staff morale, ergonomics, managerial issues, job satisfaction, motivation, and sick leave. Frequently they are employed by companies to enhance the satisfaction and/or performance of employees. Consumer psychologists focus on marketing issues such as advertising, shopping behaviour, market research, and the development of new products for changing markets.

People who have studied psychology often find that a grounding in the subject is useful in both their personal lives and their work. There are many advantages in knowing something about how the mind works and in knowing how to determine whether intuitions or preconceptions about its workings are justified. Both the findings of psychologists and the methods they use to discover things are potentially useful in a range of professional roles such as management and personnel, communications, marketing, teaching, social work, policing, nursing and medicine, research (e.g. for TV or radio programmes), political advising or analysis, journalism or writing, and also training or caring for animals. The discipline of psychology teaches skills that are widely applicable, as it provides training in thinking scientifically and critically as well as in research methodology and statistical analysis.

## Uses and abuses of psychology

People frequently make assumptions about what psychologists are able to do—for example, they assume that psychologists can tell what they are thinking from their body language or read their minds. While such assumptions are understandable, they are erroneous. Psychologists can, as we have seen, study aspects of thinking, use rewards to change behaviour, intervene with people who are distressed, and predict future behaviour with some accuracy. Nevertheless they cannot read people's minds or manipulate people who are free agents against their will.

Psychology can also be misused, as indeed can any other scientific body of information. Some of its misuses are relatively trivial; as in providing superficial answers to difficult questions, such as how to become a good parent; but others are not at all trivial: for example, treating people with certain political opinions as mentally ill, or using what psychologists have discovered about the effects of sensory deprivation to devise methods of torture. The fact that psychology, like any other discipline, can be misunderstood and misused does not detract from its value. However, psychology *is* in a special position because it is a subject about which everyone can express an opinion, based on personal information and subjective experience. For example, having spent many years researching various kinds of unhappiness, psychologists are now turning their attention to more positive emotions, and have conducted surveys into the happiness of women in their marriages. A representative survey of American women reported that half of those married five years or more said they were 'very happy' or 'completely satisfied' with their marriages and 10 per cent reported having had an affair during their current marriage. In contrast to this, Shere Hite, in her report on *Women and Love*, claimed that 70 per cent of women married five years or more were having affairs and 95 per cent of women felt emotionally harassed by the men they loved. Unlike the results of the first survey, these findings were widely reported in the media, and Shere Hite herself placed great weight on the results because 4,500 women had responded to her survey. However, less than 5 per cent of the people sampled responded (so we do not know the views of over 95 per cent of them), and only women belonging to women's organizations were contacted in the first place. Thus the respondents (the small percentage of women belonging to women's organizations who chose to respond to the survey) were not representative of the whole relevant population of women. This kind of reporting raises problems as we know that people have a tendency to accept information that fits with their hunches or preconceptions, and that attention is easily grabbed by startling, novel, or alarming information.

The point is that psychology is *not* about being led by hunches, and neither is it about common sense. In order properly to understand psychological findings people need to know something about how to evaluate the status and nature of the information they are given. Psychologists can, and do, contribute to debates such as those about marriages and related happiness, and they can help us to ask the kinds of questions that can be answered using scientific methods. Not 'Are marriages happy?' but 'What do women who have been married five years or more report about the happiness of their marriages?' The scientific, methodological nature of the study of psychology therefore determines what psychology is for—hence the importance of developing appropriate methods of inquiry, reporting results in demonstrably objective ways, and also educating others about the discipline of psychology.

Like any science, the nature of psychology has been, and is being, determined by the scientific methods and technology at its disposal. As techniques for measuring the workings of a living human brain—brain imaging techniques—have been developed, psychologists have been able to study the brain directly and begin to link changes in its functioning to the psychological phenomena of thoughts, feelings, and behaviours. Developments in computer technology help psychologists to carry out sophisticated, random sampling procedures, and to check that the samples they study are truly representative of the population in which they are interested. For example, response rates should not differ between important subgroups: for example, providing fewer responses from older people when studying the whole population. A sample of equal numbers of Caucasian and non-Caucasian people would be as unrepresentative in Zambia as it would in Russia. Statistical considerations are paramount, and these suggest, for example, that a random sample of 1,500 people could provide a reasonably accurate estimate of the views of 100 million people—provided it was representative. Having 4,500 people in the survey does not make it more accurate than a sample of 1,500 people if the composition of the sample differs in important ways from that of the population about whom conclusions are drawn. Once again the field of psychology is in an especially difficult position because some of its tools are widely available. Anyone can conduct a survey but knowing how to do it properly is a different matter.

## What next? Progress and complexity

A hundred years ago psychology as we know it today hardly existed. Great advances have been made in all aspects of the subject—and more can be expected. For example, we now know that, to a large extent, we construct our experience of the world and our understanding of what happens in it, and do not just use our faculties of perception, attention, learning, and memory to provide us with a passive reflection of external reality. Our mental life turns out to be far more active than was supposed by the early psychologists who began by documenting its structures and functions, and it has been shaped over the millennia by evolutionary forces of adaptation to be this way. Psychologists have enabled us to understand the basics about how mental processes work, and some of the basics about why they work in the way that they do. But as well as providing answers, their findings continue to raise questions. If memory is an activity not a repository, how do we understand its dynamics? Why do intelligent beings use so many illogical ways of thinking and reasoning? Can we simulate thinking to create artificially 'intelligent' machines that process prodigious quantities of information—a brain is said to include a trillion moving parts—and also help us to understand other, more human, aspects of mental life? How can we understand the processes involved in creative or non-verbal thinking and communication? What is the precise nature of the relationships between language and thought, and between thoughts and feelings? How do people change their minds? Or modify outdated or unhelpful patterns of thinking? We know that answers to these questions, and many more like them, will be complex as so many factors influence psychological aspects of functioning, but as increasingly powerful techniques of research and analysis are being developed, and as relevant variables are sorted from irrelevant ones, answers become increasingly likely.

A surprising amount of psychologists' work has been stimulated by social and political problems. For example, strides were made in the understanding and measurement of intelligence and personality during the Second World War, when the armed forces needed better means of recruitment and selection. The behaviour of people in wartime provoked Milgram's famous studies on obedience. Social deprivation in large cities provided the context for the Head Start project, from which we have learned about compensating for environmental disadvantages in early childhood. Developing business as well as political cultures provides the context for studies of leadership, team working, and goal setting. The collapse of the American energy company Enron in 2001 (the largest bankruptcy in American history at the time) prompted a series of studies on the problem of dishonesty. Obvious social problems have produced an urgent need to understand more about prejudice and about how to deal with the stresses and strains of modern life. Following riots in London in 2011 researchers have explored the effects of social networking (amongst other variables) on crowd attitudes and behaviour, and have been able to find out more about the motivation and moment-to-moment behaviour of different subgroups of those involved. It is likely that the development of psychology in the next century will continue to be influenced by the social and environmental problems we face. Psychologists are now working together with others interested in cognitive-neuroscience to discover how the brain works. However, in the early stages of research each breakthrough seems to raise more questions than it answers. The product of research is often to refine the questions that guide future hypotheses.

Psychology is a far more diverse and scientific a subject than it was even 50 years ago. Its complexity means that it may never develop as a science with a single paradigm, but it will continue to provide an understanding of mental life from many different perspectives—cognitive and behavioural, psychophysiological, biological, and social. Like any other discipline, it is the site of conflicting theories as well as consensus, which makes it an exciting discipline within which to work. For example, the more experimental and the more humanistic branches of psychology separated long ago, and have largely developed separately. Perhaps one of the more exciting challenges for psychologists today is in bringing together the products of some of its different specializations. This kind of endeavour has contributed to the development of 'cognitive science', in which scientists from many different fields, not just psychology, are now working together to further our understanding of mental functions—of brain *and* behaviour. Psychologists have always been interested in the biological basis of human life and behaviour, and are now contributing to a developing understanding of how genetics *and* the environment—nature and nurture—interact.

Close collaboration between research psychologists and their colleagues in applied fields also opens up exciting possibilities. To mention just two of these: first, advances in the understanding of how memories of stressful or traumatic events are encoded and stored has led to advances in the alleviation of conditions such as post-traumatic stress disorder by psychological interventions. Early claims that were once not testable are becoming testable, as different branches of psychology come together and inform each other. Second, research on determinants of honesty and dishonesty shows that cheating can be potentially decreased by reminding people of acceptable moral standards at the time they are facing temptation. Various reminders were tested by Ariely and his colleagues, including trying to recall the ten commandments, signing an honour code, and signing the top of a form before completing it, rather than completing it first and then signing it at the bottom. All of these methods decreased dishonest reporting, and they suggest ways of reducing cheating in academic tests, tax evasion, insurance fraud, and even false reporting of golf scores. Undoubtedly future research will raise as many questions as it answers and, equally certainly, psychology will continue to fascinate people who know about it only from their own subjective experience as well as those who make it their life's work.

# References

## Chapter 1: What is psychology? How do you study it?

James, W. (1890/1950). *The Principles of Psychology* (vol. i). New York, Dover.

Miller, G. A. (2003). The Cognitive Revolution: A Historical Perspective. *TRENDS in Cognitive Sciences*, 7(3): 141–4.

## Chapter 2: What gets into our minds? Perception

Frith, C. (2007). *Making up the Mind: How the Brain Creates Our Mental World*. Oxford, Blackwell.

Ramachadran, V. S., and Rogers-Ramachandran, D. (2004). Illusions. *Scientific American Special: Mind*, 14(1): 100–3.

Sacks, O. (1985). *The Man Who Mistook His Wife for a Hat*. London, Gerald Duckworth & Co. Ltd. (Picador, 1986).

## Chapter 3: What stays in the mind? Learning and memory

Bandura, A., and Walters, R. H. (1963). *Social Learning and Personality Development*. Orlando, FL, Holt, Rhinehart & Winston.

Bartlett, F. C. (1932). *Remembering*. Cambridge, Cambridge University Press.

Luria, A. R. (1968). *The Mind of a Mnemonist* (trans. L. Soltaroff). New York, Basic Books.

Maguire, E. A., Woollett, K., and Spiers, H. J. (2006). London Taxi Drivers and Bus Drivers: A Structural MRI and Neuropsychological Analysis. *Hippocampus*, 16: 1091–101.

Woollett, K., and Maguire, E. A. (2011). Acquiring 'the Knowledge' of London's Layout Drives Structural Brain Changes. *Current Biology*, 21: 2109–14.

## Chapter 4: How do we use what is in the mind? Thinking, reasoning, and communicating

Bateson, M., Nettle, D., and Roberts, G. (2006). Cues of Being Watched Enhance Co-operation in a Real-world Setting. *Biology Letters*, 2: 412–14.

Ernest-Jones, M., Nettle, M., and Bateson, M. (2011). Effects of Eye Images on Everyday Cooperative Behaviour: A Field Experiment. *Evolution and Human Behavior*, 32: 172–8.

Kahneman, D. (2011). *Thinking Fast and Slow*. London, Allen Lane.

Levine, M. (1971). Hypothesis Theory and Non-learning Despite Ideal S–R Reinforcement Contingencies. *Psychological Review*, 78: 130–40.

Miura, I. T., Okamoto, Y., Kim, C.-C., Chang, C.-M., et al. (1994). Comparisons of Children's Representation of Number: China, France, Japan, Korea, Sweden and the United States. *International Journal of Behavioral Development*, 17: 401–11.

Pinker, S. (2007). *The Stuff of Thought: Language as a Window into Human Nature*. London, Allen Lane.

## Chapter 5: Why do we do what we do? Motivation and emotion

Frith, C. (2007). *Making up the Mind: How the Brain Creates Our Mental World*. Oxford, Blackwell.

Latham, G. P., and Yukl, G. A. (1975). Assigned versus Participative Goal Setting with Educated and Uneducated Woods Workers. *Journal of Applied Psychology*, 60: 299–302.

Miller, G. (1967). *Psychology: The Science of Mental Life*. London, Penguin Books.

Schachter, S., and Singer, J. R. (1962). Cognitive, Social and Physiological Determinants of Emotional State. *Psychological Review*, 69: 379–99.

Schultz, W. (2001). Reward Signalling by Dopamine Neurons. *Neuroscientist*, 7(4): 293–302.

# Chapter 6: Is there a set pattern? Developmental psychology

Bowlby, J. (1951). Maternal Care and Mental Health. World Health Organization Monograph Series No. 2. Geneva, World Health Organization.

Erikson, Erik H. (1968). *Identity, Youth and Crisis*. New York, Norton.

Harlow, H. F. (1958). *American Psychologist*, 13: 673–85.

Koluchova, J. (1972). Severe Deprivation in Twins: A Case Study. *Journal of Child Psychology and Psychiatry*, 13: 107–11.

Koluchova, J. (1991). Severely Deprived Twins after 22 Years' Observation. *Studia Psychologica*, 33: 23–8.

McCrink, K., and Wynn K. (2004). Large-Number Addition and Subtraction by 9-Month-Old Infants. *Psychological Science*, 15(11): 776–81.

Nyberg, L., Lövdén, M., Riklund, K., Lindenberger, U., and Bäckman, L. (2012). Memory Aging and Brain Maintenance. *Trends in Cognitive Sciences*, 16(5): 292–305.

Reddy, V. (2007). Getting Back to the Rough Ground: Deception and 'Social Living'. *Philosophical Transactions of the Royal Society*, 362(1480): 621–37.

Starkey, P., Spelke, E. S., and Gelman, R. (1990). Numerical Abstraction by Human Infants. *Cognition*, 36: 97–128.

Steinberg, L. (2008). A Social Neuroscience Perspective on Adolescent Risk-Taking. *Developmental Review*, 28(1): 78–106.

# Chapter 7: Can we categorize people? Individual differences

Cattell, R. B. (1963). Theory of Fluid and Crystallized Intelligence: A Critical Experiment. *Journal of Educational Psychology*, 54: 1–22.

Deary, I. J. (2001). *Intelligence: A Very Short Introduction*. Oxford, Oxford University Press.

Eysenck, H. J. (1965). *Fact and Fiction in Psychology*. Harmondsworth, Penguin Books Ltd.

# Chapter 8: What happens when things go wrong? Abnormal psychology

American Psychiatric Association (2013). *Diagnostic and Statistical Manual of Mental Disorders* (5th edition). Arlington, VA: American Psychiatric Publishing.

Roth, A., and Fonagy, P. (2005). *What Works for Whom? A Critical Review of Psychotherapy Research* (2nd edition). New York, Guilford.

Westbrook, D., Kennerley, H., and Kirk, J. (2007). *An Introduction to Cognitive Behaviour Therapy: Skills and Application*. London, Sage.

## Chapter 9: How do we influence each other? Social psychology

Aronson, E., and Osherow, N. (1980). Co-operation, Pro-social Behaviour and Academic Performance: Experiments in the Desegregated Classroom. *Applied Social Psychology Annual*, 1: 163–96.

Asch, S. E. (1955). Opinions and Social Pressure. *Scientific American*, 193: 35.

Hogg, M. A., and Vaughan, G. M. (2007). *Social Psychology* (5th edition). Harlow, Pearson Education Ltd.

Kassin, S. M., Fein, S., and Markus, H. R. (2014). *Social Psychology*, 9th Edition. Belmont, CA, Wadsworth.

Milgram, S. (1974). *Obedience to Authority: An Experimental View*. New York, Harper & Row.

Sherif, M., Harvey, O. J., White, B. J., Hood, W. R., and Sherif, C. W. (1961). *Intergroup Conflict and Co-operation: The Robbers' Cave Experiment*. Norman, OK, University of Oklahoma Press.

# Further reading

Psychology is a fast developing subject, and new books become available each month. So check for new editions before buying textbooks, and keep an eye out for more recent general books, especially those receiving good reviews. Here is a short list of books we currently recommend.

Ariely, D. (2012). *The Honest Truth about Dishonesty*. London, HarperCollins.

Baddeley, A., Eysenck, M. W., and Anderson, M. C. (2009). *Memory*. London, Psychology Press.

Bowlby, J. (1997). *Attachment and Loss* (vol. i, 2nd edition). London, Century.

Burns, T. (2013). *Our Necessary Shadow*. London, Penguin Press.

Butler, G., and Hope, T. (2007). *Manage Your Mind: The Mental Fitness Guide* (2nd edition). Oxford, Oxford University Press.

Chabris, C., and Simons, D. (2010). *The Invisible Gorilla*. London, HarperCollins.

Dunbar, R., Lycett, J., and Barrett, L. (2007). *Evolutionary Psychology: A Beginner's Guide*. Oxford, Oneworld Publications.

Freeman, D., and Freeman, J. (2010). *Use Your Head: A Guided Tour of the Human Mind*. London, John Murray.

Frith, C. (2007). *Making up the Mind: How the Brain Creates our Mental World*. Oxford, Blackwell.

Goleman, D. (1996). *Emotional Intelligence*. London, Bloomsbury.

Gross, R. D. (2012). *Key Studies in Psychology* (6th edition). London, Hodder & Stoughton.

Gross, R. D. (2010). *Psychology: The Science of Mind and Behaviour* (6th edition). London, Hodder & Stoughton.

Kahneman, D. (2011). *Thinking Fast and Slow*. London, Allen Lane.

Myers, D. G. (2012). *Psychology* (10th edition). London, Worth Publishers.

Papalla, D., Olds, S., and Feldman, R. (2008). *Human Development*. New York, McGraw Hill.

Pinker, G. S. (1997). *How the Mind Works*. New York, W. W. Norton & Co.

Seligman, M. (2011). *Flourish: A New Understanding of Happiness and Well-Being—And How to Achieve Them*. London, Nicholas Brealey Publishing.

Thompson, C. (2013). *Smarter Than You Think: How Technology is Changing Our Minds for the Better*. London, William Collins.

Wegner, D. M. (2002). *The Illusion of Conscious Will*. Cambridge, MA, Bradford Books.

Winston, R. (2003). *The Human Mind and How to Make the Most of It*. London, Bantam Press.

Psychology

# Index

Index

# Expand your collection of
# VERY SHORT INTRODUCTIONS